THE JOY OF SOARING

THE JOY OF
SOARING
A TRAINING MANUAL

Written by

Carle Conway

Illustrations by

Gil Parcell

The Soaring Society of America, Inc.
Los Angeles, California

CONTENTS

PART II — SOARING

APPENDICES

FOREWORD

The title of this book, "The Joy of Soaring— A Training Manual" may seem at first glance to be a contradiction, but this is not the case. Proper training and practice are prerequisites for proficiency in any activity and this is as true for soaring as it is for playing a musical instrument, for example. Gliding is a pleasure from the very start, but the relaxation that comes from flying well and safely adds immeasurably to the enjoyment.

The tremendous surge of interest in soaring which took place in the United States during the middle sixties brought thousands of new pilots into the sport, and caused a large increase in the number of operators of soaring sites and schools. Some of these schools developed their own training manuals but there was not much uniformity among these teaching aids and there was no training manual generally available to all soaring pilots, such as the one put out by the FAA for power pilot training. The second chapter of SSA's American Soaring Handbook covers training methods, but it is primarily a syllabus for teaching rather than a manual for the student. This volume is published by SSA primarily for the student.

As part of the preparation of this manual, its author visited numerous gliding schools from coast to coast in order to ensure that the text represented the best practices of commercial and club schools, as well as to hear the ideas of many prominent soaring pilots. He soon became aware that different ways of teaching and performing some of the maneuvers in the curriculum were being practiced with apparent success at different schools and clubs. A policy decision had to be made whether to explain *all* these concepts or to take a more selective approach. In order to avoid confusing the student, it was decided to take the latter course. In some cases, actual instruction of groups of students using different concepts was undertaken on a comparative basis to determine which approach was better both from the viewpoint of the instructor and the student. As a result of this program, and the many conferences which preceded each decision, the SSA is confident that the manual will be a highly effective guide for all concerned. At the same time it is recognized that there are other ways of doing things, and no school or club should feel under the least obligation to alter methods which have been satisfactory in the past.

Part I of this manual is devoted to teaching the beginner to fly a glider and the rated power pilot to learn the differences between gliding and powered flight. Part II tells how to use this new knowledge to master the art of soaring. There are concepts and discussions that will be as valuable to the experienced pilot as to the novice. There is much material that is new to the literature of soaring; it is far from being yesterday's dinner warmed over.

The SSA is greatly indebted to the several advisors who contributed so much time and thought to make this volume as valuable as possible. Particular thanks go to Carle Conway and Gil Parcell who gave unstintingly of their time and energy for the same purpose, so that you, the reader, may share with them the joy of soaring.

HARNER SELVIDGE
*SSA Training Manual
Project Manager*

ABOUT THE AUTHOR

Carle Conway earned his pilot's license in 1928 and has been flying ever since, both as an amateur and professional. During World War II he was an instructor in the Air Force and later a Squadron Commander in the Air Transport Command hauling gas from India to China.

Mr. Conway holds a commercial license with single and multi-engine, land and sea, instrument and instructor ratings. His glider pilot's license is commercial with flight instructor rating. He holds U.S. Gold Badge with three diamonds #81.

ACKNOWLEDGMENTS

This training manual had its genesis in a suggestion by Mrs. Catherine Hiller, SSA Governor for Massachusetts. As a member of the FAA Woman's Advisory Committee for Aeronautics she proposed that FAA publish a glider training manual similar to the one they have for power pilots, and that it be prepared for FAA by the SSA. Budget restrictions prevented prompt action by FAA, so SSA undertook the complete job of preparation and publishing on its own.

The real authors of this manual are the operators and instructors of the following schools and clubs as well as the other individual pilots who gave so generously of their time and experience to make this manual possible and even authoritative. They made the effort for love of the sport of soaring and their contribution will help others to the enjoyment of it.

Briegleb Soaring School, El Mirage, Calif.
Great Western Soaring School, Pearblossom, Calif.
Schweizer Soaring School, Elmira, N.Y.
Soaring Society of Dayton, Inc., Dayton, Ohio
Texas Soaring Association, Grand Prairie, Texas
Sky Sailing Airport, Fremont, Calif.
Wave Flights, Inc., Colorado Springs, Colo.

Julian H. Allen	Henry G. Combs	Frederick J. Robinson
Leslie Arnold	Anthony Doherty	Ernest Schweizer
Paul Bikle	Stephen Doherty	Paul Schweizer
Ross Briegleb	Stephen duPont	William Schweizer
Edward H. Butts	James F. Hurst	Harner Selvidge
H. Marshall Claybourn	David Johnson	Bernald S. Smith
Bernard Carris	Erwin Jones	Sterling Starr
George E. Coder	Charles Kirschner	Graham Thomson

Robert Slater helped by editing and Gil Parcell, who is artist and glider instructor combined, did the illustrations and the beautiful painting for the dust jacket. The photographs which show so much of the beauty of soaring are by Alex Aldott, George Uveges and Linn Emrich. Thornton Ladd took all these ingredients and designed the easy-to-read and attractive layout of the book. The whole soaring community including the writer owes all these good people a debt of gratitude. Thank you, every one.

CARLE CONWAY

April 30, 1969

PART I   GLIDING

1. THE INTRODUCTORY FLIGHT

Most schools and glider clubs offer introductory rides at reduced rates. The passengers show every degree of interest from the couldn't-care-less girl friend of an enthusiast to the bona fide prospective glider pilot. Many of these passengers fall in love with the sport and ultimately earn their soaring wings.

The reason for discussing the introductory flight is that the student-to-be will probably never again have a flight on which he will learn so much. It is *all* new. Simply by keeping his eyes open, the passenger will inevitably absorb a great deal about how gliders are managed on the ground and in the air.

He also discovers his own reaction to soaring. This is the critical factor that determines whether he will pursue the sport. Unfortunately, no single flight can show him the ever-changing character of the atmosphere which provides the spice of variety for soaring. Today the stable air provides a glide of silky smoothness—but no lift. Tomorrow the air may be unstable and the hot sunshine will produce thermals that carry the glider up a thousand feet in a minute. Hopefully, the pilot is himself an enthusiast and will tell his passenger about the infinite variety and the quality of the unexpected which challenge and fascinate sailplane pilots.

Many introductory ride passengers feel concern about gliding such as appears in the following typical conversation:

Question: "What do you do when you can't find any up-currents?"

Answer: "Right now, I would land at the airport. It's within easy gliding range."

Question: "What if you are flying cross-country and there isn't any airport within gliding range?"

Answer: "Airports are not absolutely essential for landing a glider. There are many other safe fields. We keep one of these within range at all times. It's something like crossing a stream on stepping stones. You don't leave the one you are on unless you can easily jump to the next. From here, I can see three fields that would be easy to land in. (Pointing), there, there, and that smaller one over there."

Question: "Isn't that last one pretty small? After all, there's no second chance without a motor."

At last we have the heart of the matter: no motor and small field. The passenger's expression reflects his anxiety at the mere thought. This question has come up so often that the pilot knows how to field it. He explains the glider's capability of glide path control, of accurate spot landing, of moderate speed at touchdown and short roll-out. Later, when he returns to the airport, he points out in advance his planned landing spot and then proves the truth of his explanation by landing on it. He makes it seem easy because it *is* easy. This demonstration usually sets to rest this one principal worry about the safety of motorless flight.

Schweizer 2-33s, most-used American trainers — photo by Alex Aldott

2. THEORY OF GLIDER FLIGHT

WING, FUSELAGE AND TAIL

Most gliders consist of three basic components: the wing, the fuselage, and the tail surfaces. The wing supports the glider, and the ailerons and tail surfaces provide stability and control. The fuselage performs the dual function of holding the wing and tail in proper relationship to each other and of providing cockpit space for the pilot. If one understands how the wing functions, the rest of the theory of glider flight follows naturally and logically. Understanding helps in learning the practical techniques of flight.

The way a wing works is not obvious, compared, for example, to the functioning of a wheel on a car. A wheel can be seen turning, bearing against the solid earth to apply power or to change direction. The wing works invisibly in an atmosphere that yields before the passage of the glider. But the air has substance and offers resistance, supporting the wing even as it gives way to it.

What the wing does is to drive a mass of air downward, producing an equal and opposite upward reaction upon itself in accord with Newton's 3rd law of motion. (Oddly enough, under most conditions the top of the wing contributes far more to this action than the bottom, which explains why glider pilots are so particular about wiping off the tops and less finicky about the lower surface.) The upward reaction on the glider is made up of two force factors: lift, which acts upward at right angles to the direction of motion; and drag, which acts rearward, or parallel to the direction of motion. The values of these two forces, expressed as a ratio, describe the glide performance of the craft at a given time. If lift is twenty times as great as drag (expressed L/D=20:1), the glider will move forward twenty feet for each foot of altitude lost. In soaring, lift is the hero and drag is the villain.

The ability of a given wing to generate lift is in proportion to the density of the air, to speed, and to the angle at which the wing strikes the air. Denser air produces more lift because the wing has firmer substance to push against, so the reaction upon itself is greater. More speed gives more lift because the wing can deflect more air downward in a given time. Glider speed is dependent on the pull of gravity or the tug of the towrope.

The third factor in the effectiveness of a wing is the angle at which it strikes the air. This *angle of attack* is important to the pilot because he controls it directly by moving the stick fore and aft, which has the secondary effect of changing the wing's lift and drag (which means angle of descent) and the glider's airspeed.

Decreasing the angle of attack reduces lift, while increasing it generates more lift—but only up to a point. At an angle of attack in the area of 12 to 18 degrees (depending on the shape of the particular airfoil), the wing begins to lose its ability to deflect air downward and

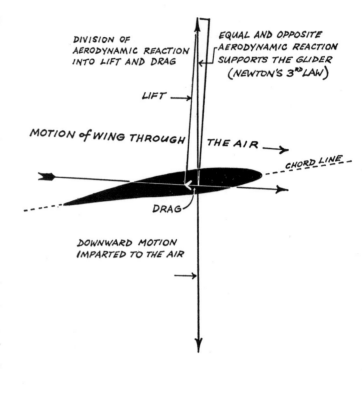

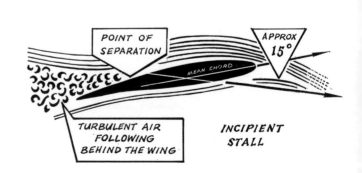

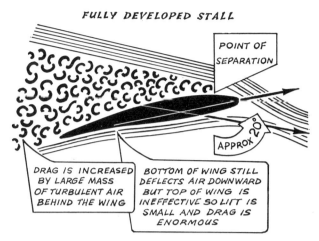

POINT OF SEPARATION

APPROX 20°

DRAG IS INCREASED BY LARGE MASS OF TURBULENT AIR BEHIND THE WING

BOTTOM OF WING STILL DEFLECTS AIR DOWNWARD BUT TOP OF WING IS INEFFECTIVE SO LIFT IS SMALL AND DRAG IS ENORMOUS

instead begins to produce a turbulent wake behind its upper surface. With only a slight additional increase in the angle of attack, lift decreases rapidly and drag builds up vastly, so the rate of sink increases; control is greatly reduced, and the wing is said to be *stalled*. (This is usually the condition with the control stick all the way back.) To regain lift, the angle of attack must be reduced (stick forward), returning the wing to the range of angles of attack where the air flows smoothly over the top surface and is deflected downward.

FUNCTIONS OF THE CONTROLS

Control surfaces are provided to allow the attitude of the glider to be changed about its three axes. The pilot can blend these three movements to produce any desired change in attitude.

Moving the stick sideways depresses one

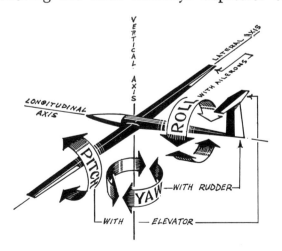

VERTICAL AXIS

LATERAL AXIS

ROLL WITH AILERONS

LONGITUDINAL AXIS

PITCH

YAW —WITH RUDDER—

—WITH — ELEVATOR—

aileron and raises the other, making the lift of the two wings unequal and rolling the glider right or left around the axis of the fuselage. Other results also appear which will be discussed later in this chapter, when we take up turning.

The vertical and horizontal tail surfaces are small airfoils which work like the wing to deflect the airflow and so produce equal and opposite reactions upon themselves. Moving the stick fore and aft moves the elevator and lowers or raises the nose of the glider so long as airspeed is adequate. A less superficial description of this action is that the elevator controls the angle of attack of the wing.

The rudder pedals are connected to the rudder in such a way that pushing the left pedal moves the glider's nose to the left. This may not seem logical when compared to the way a sled is steered; however, the use of the rudder is *not* to steer the glider but to align its fuselage so as to minimize (and occasionally to maximize) its drag. For this reason, the logic of steering is unimportant; the rudder simply yaws the glider around its vertical axis.

STABILITY

Stability of direction and bank are interrelated and complicated subjects of more interest to designers than to pilots. Few gliders will return to a wings-level glide without help from the pilot; in fact, few will long remain in that condition if left to themselves. For good reason, designers rely on the pilot to handle directional and banking stability.

Pitch stability, possessed by gliders in widely varying degrees, is of great interest to the pilot. This quality appears as a resistance on the part of the craft to flight at speeds other than that for which it is trimmed. If trimmed for 40 mph, for example, the pilot might have to exert a strong forward pressure on the stick to fly at 80 mph. Should he relax the pressure the glider would, after a series of pitch oscillations, return to 40 mph.

Gliders with high pitch stability require elevator trimming devices either on the control surface or adjustable springs in the control system to permit the pilot to fly the glider at any reasonable speed without having to hold a steady pressure on the stick. A few glider models have been deliberately designed with neutral stability and do not generate a stick load by changing speed. These gliders do not require a trimmer.

GLIDE PATH AND SPEED CONTROLS

When making an approach for a landing the pilot must be able to steepen his glide without gaining speed. He also needs a means to check his speed when diving to lose altitude rapidly. Several of the devices for providing this control are of interest to all glider pilots.

Spoilers, which are used on most training gliders, are devices of various styles, some perforated, which emerge from the top or bottom of the wing, or both. They may be hinged or may slide out vertically from slots in the general vicinity of the main spar. The prime purpose of spoilers is to break up the smooth flow of air over a portion of the wing, "spoiling" the lift. Secondarily, drag is increased. (Recall that L/D determines the angle of descent.)

Dive brakes are devices whose primary purpose is to increase drag. Most dive brakes are a part of the wing, and so also decrease lift. The choice of names depends on whether the accent is on decreasing lift (spoilers) or increasing drag (dive brakes). Fuselage dive brakes and drogue parachutes have no direct effect on lift, working entirely by increasing drag.

Since there are a number of sailplanes available which have drogue parachutes as supplements to spoilers and flaps, it should be noted that they are extremely effective speed-limiting devices. However, their functioning in gliders has not been 100% reliable, and a failure to open usually comes at the most in-

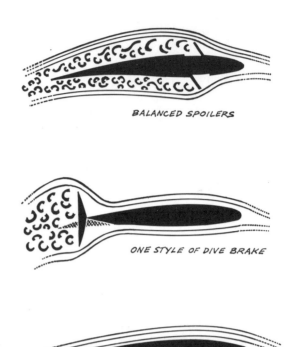

BALANCED SPOILERS

ONE STYLE OF DIVE BRAKE

ONE STYLE OF FLAP

FOWLER FLAP (TRACKS NOT SHOWN) LARGE INCREASE IN AREA AND LIFT SMALLER INCREASE IN DRAG. REDUCES MINIMUM SPEED.

convenient moment. Further, once deployed, they cannot be controlled or retracted and redeployed. Another handicap is that the backward pull of the chute upon the tail of the glider substantially reduces the effectiveness of both rudder and elevator. Perhaps these problems will one day be solved; meanwhile, too much reliance should not be placed upon the drogue parachute.

Flaps, which are used on some gliders, work differently from spoilers. Flaps are hinged portions of the trailing edge of the wing that, when lowered, change the camber or cross-sectional curvature of the wing so as to increase both lift and drag. One type of flap has moderate up and down travel for high-speed cruising and thermaling; the function of speed control is handled by separate spoilers. Another type of flap functions in the same way for cruising and thermaling, but dispenses with the supplementary spoiler, powerful drag being provided by lowering the flap as much as 90 degrees to the chord line.

Several models of gliders have Fowler flaps, similar to those used on many airliners. Fowler flaps lower and at the same time slide backward on tracks so as to increase the area of the wing, to change its camber, and to provide a slot which smooths the airflow on the top surface of the flap. The Fowler flap increases drag moderately when partly extended for thermaling, and very greatly when fully depressed for speed control.

All the above devices tend to reduce speed, other factors remaining the same, and may be designed to keep *maximum* diving speed at a safe figure; they are then called "terminal velocity limiting."

EFFECT OF AIR DENSITY ON PERFORMANCE

The density of the air becomes less as altitude and temperature increase. In thinner air a wing must be driven faster to produce a given amount of lift, all other things being unchanged. Fortunately, a change in air density affects the airspeed indicator in the same way as it does the wing, since they both function by the dynamic reaction of the air. Therefore, a pilot can rely on the airspeed indicator under most conditions without making a correction for density. Stalling speed, redline speed, and glide ratios throughout the performance range of the glider are constant in terms of airspeed indicator readings. True airspeed, which is the indicated airspeed corrected for the density factor (disregarding the question of instrumental error), has a bearing on cross-country strategy and the possibility of flutter; its use in navigation is *nil* because of the irregular gait by which gliders wend their way across the land.

EFFECT OF LOADING ON PERFORMANCE

A heavily loaded glider goes forward *and down* faster than when lightly loaded. The glide ratios are the same for both loading conditions, but occur at different airspeeds. This may seem strange until one realizes that an increase in weight does not affect either lift or drag, the determining factors of glide ratio. Unfortunately, *all* the airspeeds on the performance curve of the heavily-loaded glider are higher, including stalling speed, and worst of all from the soaring standpoint, the range of thermaling speeds.

On a normal cross-country flight the heavily loaded glider makes better time between thermals but takes longer to regain the altitude lost. Both its minimum thermaling circle and its rate of sink (because of the steeper bank required) are greater than for a lightly loaded glider. When the thermals are strong the "lead sled" runs away from the "floater." When the thermals are weak, the floaters stay up and make progress while the heavy jobs are fighting simply to stay up, or perhaps are unable to do so.

Jettisonable water ballast is carried in some gliders in an effort to combine the best qualities of both types. This solution is incomplete, however, since water cannot be taken on in flight when thermals strengthen in the early afternoon.

As things stand now, no glider is ideal under all conditions. Each type is designed for certain assumed conditions and represents the designer's idea of the best compromise between speed and thermaling ability.

THE TURN

Newton's first law of motion (loosely stated) says that a moving body will keep moving in the same direction until a force acts to turn it. The force that turns the glider is the lift of the wing.

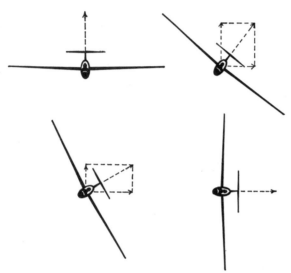

HOW BANKING DIRECTS THE LIFT TO TURN THE GLIDER

In level flight, wing lift works upward, supporting the glider but not turning it. By banking the craft, some of the lift is stolen for the purpose of overcoming inertia and centrifugal force and so pulling the glider around the turn. The proportional part of the lift devoted to turning and the part still devoted to vertical support vary with the angle of bank, as can be graphically described by the familiar parallelogram of forces.

While turning, the pilot must increase *total* lift so the proportional part supporting the glider continues adequate for the task. Speed, angle of attack, or both must be increased. These changes also increase total drag and steepen the glide path. Thus, a steeper bank results in a higher sink rate, an important fact to remember in the art of thermaling.

The correct way to bank a glider is with the ailerons and rudder, the rudder being used en-tirely to keep the fuselage streamlined. The wrong way to bank is with the rudder alone. Should a pilot push right rudder leaving the ailerons neutral, the fuselage would pivot to the right causing the wings to bank to the right. The lift of the wing in the banked attitude would then produce a right turn. This procedure is faulty for two reasons. The first concerns the high drag set up by the skidding fuselage which causes loss of altitude. The second concerns the effect if the wing is close to stalling, when the skidding turn may put the glider in a spin.

UNDESIRED SIDE EFFECTS OF THE TURN

In turning a glider, the pilot must counter-act five undesired side effects, undesired in the sense that if they did not already exist, the designer would not design them into the aircraft. During student training, the development of habit patterns to overcome these side effects, is perhaps the largest single factor in learning to fly. Success will be much easier when the student understands the causes behind his vexations.

The first side effect is called *adverse yaw*, and is encountered when banking into or out of a turn. To roll into a left turn, for example, the pilot depresses the right aileron and raises the left one. Since the down aileron produces more drag than the other, an undesirable yawing to the right (against the direction of the turn) takes place, generating unwanted drag as the fuselage moves sideways through

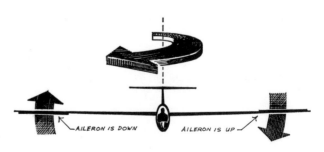

AILERON IS DOWN   AILERON IS UP

ADVERSE YAW

the air. To balance out this adverse yaw and so streamline the fuselage, the pilot applies left rudder with the left aileron. This action is called "coordinating stick and rudder", and the result is called a properly coordinated turn when the yaw string and the slip-skid ball are centered.

Adverse yaw is mild at low angles of attack but becomes severe when the wing is nearly stalled. For example, in a tight turn which is close to an accelerated stall, the application of full aileron to roll out can stall the low wingtip. The severe drag on this wing yaws the glider into a dive. If the pilot now makes the understandable error of trying to raise the glider's nose by pulling the stick even farther back the result will be a sudden spin. To recover from such an excessively tight turn, the angle of attack must first be reduced by moving the stick forward, followed by coordinated use of aileron and rudder to level the wings. A normal rollout results.

The *diving tendency* is the second "I wish it wouldn't happen" in a turn. When the glider is banked some of the wing's lift is transferred from the task of support to that of pulling the glider around the turn, as previously explained. In consequence, the rate of sink increases, stabilizing action causes the glider's nose to drop, and the airspeed increases. If the pilot does not oppose this reaction of the glider by moving the stick back, the airspeed will soon stabilize at a higher level than formerly. To maintain the same speed in the turn as in straight flight the pilot must use the elevator to keep the nose at such a position on the horizon as to hold that speed. The steeper the bank, the more back pressure on the control stick is needed.

The *overbanking tendency* is the third annoyance in turning. Having established the desired angle of bank, the pilot finds that he has to hold top aileron (against the angle of bank) to keep the bank from steepening. In a glider

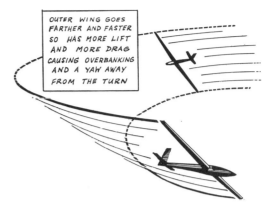

OUTER WING GOES FARTHER AND FASTER SO HAS MORE LIFT AND MORE DRAG CAUSING OVERBANKING AND A YAW AWAY FROM THE TURN

OVERBANKING TENDENCY AND YAW IN A TURN

this is true in all but the shallowest banks because of the long span and normally small radius of turn. The outer wingtip moves faster than the inner, so the outer wing has more lift, causing the bank to steepen.

The fourth unwanted side effect, a *yaw against the direction of an established turn* (not the adverse yaw caused by aileron drag) appears because the faster-moving outer wing has more drag. Opposite rudder is needed to balance the wing's yawing force, the amount being indicated by the yaw string or slip-skid ball. If these are centered the turn is correctly coordinated, even though the controls are "crossed", which means rudder is applied on one side and aileron on the other. "Crossed controls" is a heinous sin in powered flight. Power pilots please note that a glider is flown so the fuselage slips through the air with minimum drag, ball in the center, whatever position of the controls is required to accomplish this end. No spin will result since the drags of wing and rudder balance one another.

The fifth and last (thank goodness) side effect of turning is the *increase in stalling speed*. As was explained earlier, during a turn the pilot applies back pressure on the stick to increase the angle of attack. Thus the glider is closer to a stalled angle than in a level glide at the same speed. Another way to look at the

9

situation is that the load of centrifugal force is added to the weight of the glider; this higher total load on the wing raises the stalling speed. The thermaling pilot soon learns that he has to increase his airspeed as he steepens his bank in order to keep from stalling. It should be noted that the increase in stalling speed is caused by the increased wing loading rather than by the angle of bank *per se*. In the performance of aerobatic maneuvers such as a wingover the bank may be vertical and the stick is not brought back; there is no turning and no centrifugal force, and the glider's wing is not stalled even though the glider is momentarily hanging almost motionless in a vertical bank.

The following table gives an idea of the degree to which stalling speed increases with the angle of bank in a *properly executed turn*. The percentage increase is included so the reader can calculate actual values for any glider. Figures are also given for a typical trainer and a high-performance sailplane.

Angle of Bank	"G" Load	% Increase in Stall Speed	Trainer Stalling Speed	High-performance Stalling Speed
0°	1.0	0	31	46
30°	1.18	8	33.5	50
45°	1.4	18	36.5	54
60°	2.0	40	43.5	64.5
75°	4.0	100	62	92

90° A "properly executed turn" is impossible.

EFFECT OF WINDS ON TURNS

An observant beginner pilot (with instructor) making a full-circle turn at an altitude of less than a thousand feet while under strong and steady wind conditions, will be convinced that glider turns are affected by the wind. In a downwind direction, even a steep bank produces a turn of large radius over the earth and the glider goes very fast. Turning in the upwind direction, the radius of the turn is very small and the speed is visibly slowed. The student pilot *knows* that wind affects the way the glider turns because he can *see* the effect just by watching the ground. He feels that the airspeed indicator must be wong, and that the instructor, who is saying the wind doesn't affect the way a glider turns, simply doesn't believe the evidence of his eyes.

GROUND TRACK OF A GLIDER CIRCLING IN A MOVING PARCEL OF AIR

Everything the beginner sees is "absolutely so." It is what he cannot see, which is the motion of the parcel of air in which he is flying, that leads to his incorrect conclusion. He can't even feel the strong wind that is causing his glider to behave so eccentrically compared to the expected constant-rate turn.

An analogy may clarify the situation. Consider a motorboat turning in a river. The boat, in making a constant rate turn, will soon run into its own wake, and the skipper can look around and see a trail of bubbles marking the perfectly circular course. When he looks at the shore, he finds himself downstream of where he started his circle. If during the turn the skipper had looked over the side and watched his path over the river-bottom, he would have seen the resultant of the circular motion of the boat and the straight motion of the river. It probably would never occur to him that a boat's turning capability is different in a river than on the placid surface of a lake because he can see all the elements that are involved, unlike our beginner pilot.

When turning in a high wind the pilot makes no change in his use of the controls. However, when he is concerned with his track over the ground, as when in the traffic pattern or on the cross-wind leg of a triangle flight, he must crab into the wind enough to compensate for the motion of the air.

It should be noted that *changes* in wind direction or velocity, as distinct from a steady wind, do affect the way a glider handles. Such conditions, occurring in thunderstorms, wave rotors, and in the disturbed air close to the ground are discussed at some length elsewhere in this manual.

3. ON THE GROUND

MOVING THE GLIDER

After the glider has been uncovered, pre-flighted and untied, it must be pulled to the take-off area. If the distance is considerable it will be far easier to pull the glider by car rather than by hand. The towrope should be at least as long as the glider's span. In fair weather and on a level field, one person driving and one "walking" a wingtip are sufficient. When the glider is to be moved downhill, a man will be needed at each wingtip. If it is windy, a third person may be needed to carry the tail to keep the wing at a low angle of attack or to sit in the cockpit for the same purpose. When a glider has to be moved under extreme wind conditions, the utmost care and good planning are called for. Just a moment of carelessness may allow the wind to flip the glider over or bring about an unscheduled flight.

FAIR WEATHER — ONE PERSON DRIVING — ONE AT WINGTIP

TOW-ROPE AS LONG, AT LEAST, AS GLIDER'S WING SPAN

DOWNHILL TOWING — ONE PERSON TO EACH WINGTIP

SEVERE WEATHER — EXTRA MAN TO KEEP TAIL RAISED PLUS PILOT IN COCKPIT

While being moved, and until the pilot is actually ready to enter the cockpit, the glider should be kept back from the area of landing and take-off. If there is to be a delay, it should not be left unattended unless securely tied down. Under windy conditions, a pilot should sit in the cockpit and keep the spoilers open (or flaps up), the brakes on, and the stick forward to preclude an involuntary take-off.

A parked car or two can be of help under adverse weather conditions—either as a wind-break, a temporary tie-down, or both.

Those who move gliders on an airport have the urgent responsibility of staying clear of all other activities.

GETTING SETTLED IN THE COCKPIT

Comfort is a "must" for all pilots since one can't give proper attention to the problems of flight when feeling cramped or held too tightly by the seat belt and shoulder straps.

Many gliders have adjustable rudder pedals, and these should be set so that full travel of the rudder can be accomplished without stretching or cramping the legs. In the absence of rudder pedal adjustments, the pilot must adjust his body position using pillows or a parachute.

Good visibility forward is of utmost importance, and the pilot must be sure to use enough seat cushions under him so that he can see downward over the nose of the glider as far as possible.

Before getting in the cockpit, the pilot should loosen the belt and shoulder straps to facilitate fastening and adjustment. When he is seated, the belt should be tightened first, and then the shoulder straps should be taken up firmly but not uncomfortably.

An important part of pilot comfort is maintaining a relaxed muscular state. Whenever a pilot feels tense, or is gripping the stick too hard or pushing against the rudder pedals, he should make a conscious effort to relax. Improved coordination and better piloting at less cost in fatigue will be the result.

BEFORE TAKE-OFF CHECKLIST

To err is human, to use a checklist (though not divine) is at least a safeguard against human weakness.* The usual glider checklist for use before taking off is based upon the following memory aid: A B C C C D. The initials stand for:

---

*SSA offers (at nominal cost) a pocketable glider checklist for all occasions. It represents a lot of thought, and is recommended.

TAKE-OFF CHECKLIST
A-B-C-C-C-D

ALTIMETER—Set to field elevation.

BELTS—Fasten and adjust.

CONTROLS—Check for proper operation. Close spoilers. Set flaps.

CANOPY—Close, and check latches carefully.

CABLE—Hook up, check release, and hook up again.

DIRECTION—Observe direction of the wind.

The above checklist is adequate for local soaring in most gliders. However, more ambitious flights and more complex equipment call for additional checks before take-off. For example: oxygen turned on, barograph on, radio on and checked, landing gear signal functioning, and so on.

Before a cross-country flight a well-thought-out checklist should be prepared and used before bringing the glider out to take-off position.

If for any reason the pilot should leave the cockpit after the take-off check is completed he should release the towline. Pilotless gliders have been towed into the air accidentally, but such flights have seldom ended well. More likely *never*.

4. PRACTICAL AIRWORK

HOW TO GLIDE STRAIGHT AHEAD

The intention of the glider pilot in straight flight is *to hold a constant heading in perfectly coordinated flight at a constant airspeed*. Thus three objectives must be attained to fly the glider efficiently in a straight line.

"To hold a constant heading," the pilot selects a landmark near the horizon in the direction he wants to fly and turns the glider toward it. Each time the glider turns away from the landmark the pilot makes the slight correction required to return to the heading. Thus it can be seen that *straight* actually means relatively straight, since the pilot is human and the atmosphere is turbulent. The extent of the wandering will be in proportion to changing atmospheric conditions and to the number and type of distractions that divert the pilot's attention.

"In perfectly coordinated flight" means that ailerons and rudder are always in coordination so as to prevent slips and skids. In the early days of gliding, pilots flew "by the seat of their pants," which meant that side pressures on a pilot's body told him that he was not coordinating properly. This method of flying is safe but inefficient, since small slips and skids that develop gradually cannot be detected by the pilot's sensations. Such slight errors add significantly to the glider's drag, steepening the descent. To get the best performance from his glider, the pilot must keep the yaw string or slip-skid ball centered.

"At a constant airspeed" is an ideal but unattainable goal. The same factors that make it difficult to maintain a heading do the same with respect to airspeed, and the low pitch stability of most gliders accentuates the difficulty. To maintain a constant airspeed, the nose of the glider must be maintained at a constant level with respect to the horizon, and the airspeed indicator must be checked frequently to verify that this nose position is correct. The pilot should also stay alert to the wind noise, which can announce substantial changes in speed when his attention is upon other matters. Gusts that cause the airspeed to fluctuate temporarily should be ignored. Holding a steady pitch attitude permits the pilot to watch *outside* the cockpit for other aircraft.

The common student error is to try to control airspeed by concentrating on the airspeed indicator instead of the attitude of the glider. The airspeed indicator is slow in reporting a change in speed, mostly because the speed is slow in changing. For example, the slight change in pitch attitude required to increase the speed by five mph will take several seconds to accomplish the change because of the inertia of the glider. Overcoming the glider's inertia takes time; lag in the instrument is relatively minor. Whatever the reason, the effects of chasing the indicated airspeed are to over-

control and to make out-of-phase corrections.

In the interest of minimum drag and maximum glide ratio, all corrections in the straight glide should be made unhurriedly, with the least possible movement of the controls.

LOOK BEFORE YOU TURN

HOW TO MAKE A GLIDING TURN

The first step in making a gliding turn is to look around to make sure it is safe to turn. Freeway drivers, after a few near misses, learn to look before changing lanes. Pilots cannot afford to risk collision and must, from the start of their training, discipline themselves to look around before turning.

Throughout the turn, the pilot will have better control and will insure safety if he will look about as he turns, rather than stare straight over the nose. Watching the nose of the glider while the scenery moves rapidly across the field of vision tends to confuse the pilot and makes it easy to lose track of the progress of the turn. When turning, the slip-skid ball and airspeed indicator should be consulted with only the briefest of glances. Corrections in airspeed are made while watching the attitude of the nose on the horizon, and time must be allowed for speed to stabilize before rechecking the airspeed indicator. When the slip-skid ball is out to one side it should be centered while watching it, as there is no inertia problem or lag in the instrument response. Just a touch of left stick and right rudder, or vice versa, will center the ball. The pilot should then look away from the instruments and return his attention to the attitude of the glider.

A mechanical approach to flying is not normally recommended, but since the theory of turns has been discussed, perhaps it will fortify the theoretical approach to analyze the control movements that produce a correct entry, turn and recovery.

Assume that a turn to the left is to be made. The bank in that direction is started with left stick and left rudder together. As soon as the glider begins to roll to the left, the pilot applies light back pressure to the stick, sufficient to hold the nose at the level on the horizon required to maintain the desired airspeed. As the bank steepens, the nose position should be dropped slightly because the higher drag induced by the increased angle of attack requires more pull of gravity to keep the glider from losing speed.

When the desired angle of bank is reached, stick pressure is applied toward the high wing to control the overbanking tendency; left rudder, meanwhile, is used as required to trim out the greater induced drag of the right wing and to keep the yaw string centered. As the turn continues the pilot maintains the glider at a constant attitude with respect to the horizon, while visually sweeping the entire area, but with particular care in the direction of the turn.

The pilot should clear in the opposite direction when rolling out of the turn to avoid the possibility of cutting in front of another glider circling with him. Since turning will continue as long as the glider is banked, the pilot must start decreasing the bank, coordinating the aileron and rudder, *before* he reaches his desired heading, so that wing-levelling will be

completed at the right point. As the bank is decreased, the stick is brought gradually forward—the reverse of the procedure for turn entry.

COORDINATION EXERCISES FOR TURNING

The technique of turning properly is developed and mastered through a series of in-flight coordination exercises. The student acquires the ability through practice and exacting self-criticism and the veteran pilot maintains it in the same way. Basically, the exercises involve entering turns and rolling out again, completing each turn on a predetermined heading. The exercises are progressive, being easy enough for the beginners at the start, and difficult enough for the experts in the ultimate stage.

At the elementary level, simply pick two landmarks about 90 degrees apart. Section lines are excellent. Now, slowly and smoothly enter a shallow turn and continue it until near the target landmark. Roll out on heading and pause long enough to recover from any improper use of the controls. Repeat in the other direction. The criteria for executing these turns correctly are: perfect coordination, constant airspeed, smooth application of the controls, holding a constant pitch and bank throughout the turn, accuracy in completing the turn on heading, and remembering to clear properly.

As the student's proficiency develops, both the rate of roll and the angle of bank should be increased. The next stage is to omit the pause between turns, remembering, however, that a turn has not been done properly unless its direction is reversed on target. Continue increasing the angle of bank up to 60 degrees, and the roll rate until the aileron used requires full rudder to stay perfectly coordinated. Most training gliders will need full rudder when the ailerons are from half to three-quarters of maximum deflection.

Note: Remember to clear in the direction of

the turn before banking, and in the opposite direction when rolling out; establishing the habit of proper clearing is an essential part of coordination exercises.

THE UNINTENTIONAL HIGH-SPEED SPIRAL

In the process of learning gliding turns, a beginner may fail to control the tendencies to overbank and to dive. The bank may approach the vertical and the nose of the glider may fall more than 45 degrees below the horizon; of course, speed will increase rapidly.

If the pilot then pulls the stick back in a mistaken effort to slow the glider or to bring its nose back up to the horizon, the glider will simply turn faster and the spiral will continue to steepen. The resulting increase in the angle of attack and airspeed could overload the wing to the point of structural failure.

The right way to recover from a high-speed spiral is to *relax* the back pressure on the stick, reducing the load on the wing, and at the same time to reduce the angle of bank with coordinated aileron and rudder. When the bank is less than 45 degrees the stick may be moved

slowly and gently backward, while continuing to decrease the bank.

Control pressures must be strong enough to get the job done, but smooth and gentle enough to keep stresses at a minimum.

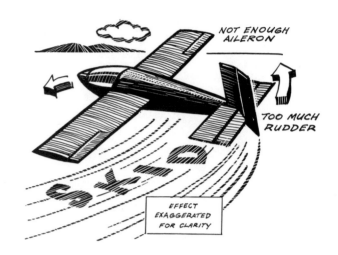

NOT ENOUGH AILERON

TOO MUCH RUDDER

SKID

EFFECT EXAGGERATED FOR CLARITY

SLIPS AND SKIDS

In a turn, a skid is caused by excessive rudder pressure in the direction of the turn disproportionate to the amount of aileron used. It causes the glider to slide outward from the turn like a skidding automobile. A slip is just the opposite, being caused by insufficient rudder in relation to the amount of aileron, which makes the glider slide inward and downward toward the center of the turn.

In straight flight, a forward slip is made by lowering a wing and holding enough rudder on the opposite side to prevent a turn.

In slips, the slip-skid ball rolls toward the low wing. In skids it rolls toward the high wing. A yaw string moves in the opposite direction.

The skid is used intentionally for entering spins. The inadvertent skid is bad technique because it creates drag and degrades the glide performance. It can also produce an accidental spin when the angle of attack is high (stick far back). Unintentional skids often result from a pilot's mistaken belief that the rudder turns the glider, as if it were a boat.

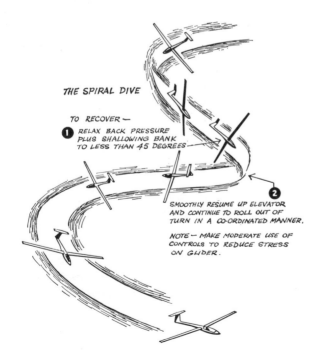

THE SPIRAL DIVE

TO RECOVER —

① RELAX BACK PRESSURE PLUS SHALLOWING BANK TO LESS THAN 45 DEGREES

② SMOOTHLY RESUME UP ELEVATOR AND CONTINUE TO ROLL OUT OF TURN IN A CO-ORDINATED MANNER.

NOTE — MAKE MODERATE USE OF CONTROLS TO REDUCE STRESS ON GLIDER.

TOO MUCH
AILERON

NOT ENOUGH
RUDDER —
OR TOP RUDDER

EFFECT
EXAGGERATED
FOR CLARITY

A slip as well as a skid can result in a spin. This occurs when the wing is stalled by bringing the stick too far back, while holding strong top rudder and bottom aileron to produce the side-slip. The spin will always be in the direction of the applied rudder. This is called an "over-the-top spin entry." The possibility of spinning out of a side-slip explains the necessity to maintain normal gliding airspeed when slipping.

The slip can be used advantageously because of the fact that it increases drag and so steepens the glide. When the angle of descent provided by spoilers is not steep enough, a side-slip will provide the extra drag to steepen it further. The glider is yawed to one side and banked to the other to the degree necessary to control the direction of motion. A steeper bank or less top rudder will result in a slipping turn.

The most frequent use of the side-slip is to counteract cross-wind drift during the final approach and landing, and during take-off. Spoil-

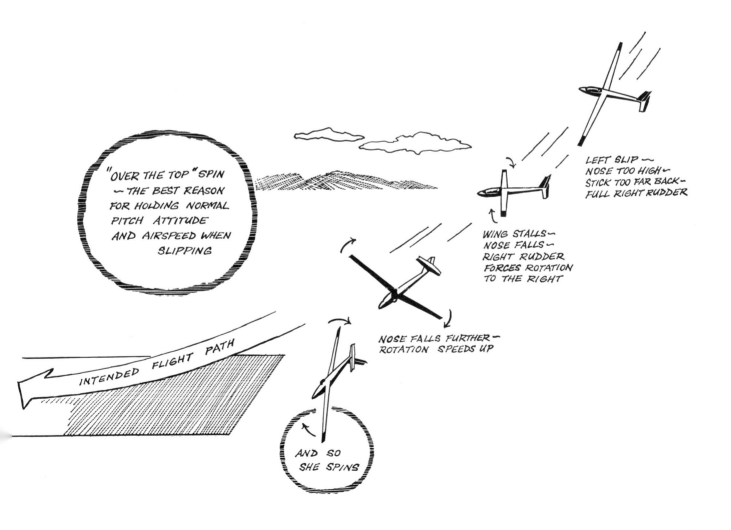

"OVER THE TOP" SPIN — THE BEST REASON FOR HOLDING NORMAL PITCH ATTITUDE AND AIRSPEED WHEN SLIPPING

LEFT SLIP — NOSE TOO HIGH — STICK TOO FAR BACK — FULL RIGHT RUDDER

WING STALLS — NOSE FALLS — RIGHT RUDDER FORCES ROTATION TO THE RIGHT

NOSE FALLS FURTHER — ROTATION SPEEDS UP

INTENDED FLIGHT PATH

AND SO SHE SPINS

ers are ordinarily adequate for approach control without slipping—unless the pilot has made a gross error in pattern planning.

Airspeed indications are not entirely accurate in slips since the air blows across the pitot tube instead of directly into it; similarly, static pressure may also be affected. During the slip, the nose is neither raised nor lowered relative to the horizon, and speed is judged by the sound of the wind. Recovery from a slip on final approach should be made in ample time to stabilize the glide attitude and approach speed before flaring out for the landing.

STALLS

Stalls are inherently harmless at any altitude sufficient for easy recovery. Not so are the accidental stalls that might occur when low. A stall below pattern entry altitude (700' to 1000') must be dealt with promptly, and above all must be prevented from developing into a spin.

Stall training consists in acquiring familiarity with the symptoms of the approaching stall and of the stall itself, and practicing the recovery until it becomes automatic. There are six indications that a stall is imminent, although they are not all present in every type of stall.

1. A nose-high attitude.
2. Lessening of wind noise.
3. Diminished indicated airspeed.
4. Less resistance of the controls; the stick feels sloppy.
5. A buffeting sound and vibration.
6. The stick is far back toward its rearward stop. This is the most reliable and consistent indication, since stalling occurs at a certain angle of attack, and stick position controls angle of attack.

These warnings, which are so prominent when practicing stalls at a safe altitude, may be less so when very close to the ground. As one well-known pilot put it: "During high-altitude stalls the glider buffets and bangs around, giving plenty of warning, and in general doesn't act the least bit vicious. On final approach the glider may drop out from under you without a whisper." This comes about because the stall is the result of external forces as well as of the pilot's misuse of the controls. A lull in the wind, the normal wind velocity gradient, or the inrush of air into the base of a thermal ahead of the glider may result in less air flowing across the wing, reducing lift. The glider sinks and the nose falls due to stabilizer action. If the pilot attempts to prevent the nose from falling by bringing back the stick (a natural reaction under the circumstances) the angle of attack may increase to the stalling point, and the stall may even develop into a spin.

The pilot's protection from these effects lies in understanding the behavior of the air close to the ground and realizing fully why he *must* maintain pattern airspeed until low enough to flare out for his landing. He should *anticipate* a decrease of airspeed on final approach and be prepared to close spoilers and nose down if that too is needed. In speed lies safety.

Stall recovery, through frequent repetition, becomes a "conditioned reflex" that responds the instant an impending or actual stall is detected. Since the training is directed toward meeting a low-altitude emergency, the recovery should be made to a wings-level, best-glide-speed attitude, with minimum possible loss of altitude. Three vigorous control movements may have to be made at the same time:

1. Stick *fully* forward,* and quickly; but don't leave it there.

---

*In the typical training glider, "stick fully forward" is unnecessary because the elevator travel is so restricted that it is difficult to force the wing to a fully-stalled angle of attack. Yet the purpose of stall training is to develop habits that will protect the pilot in the future, when he may be flying gliders with entirely different and more vigorous stall behavior. So "stick fully forward" should be the way to learn in the trainer, and the instructor should be relied upon to prevent the student from nosing the glider down beyond the angle needed to streamline the wing.

STALL RECOVERY
• STICK FORWARD
• SPOILERS CLOSED
• TOP RUDDER
FAST!

2. Spoilers closed.

3. Top rudder pedal fully forward.

The elevator usage requires some explanation. Turn back to the illustration of the wing section in a stalled condition on page 5. The drag of the stalled wing has increased astronomically since it is now pulling behind it a wake of turbulent air. This severe drag is both resisting a return to normal speed and causing a rapid loss of altitude. The wing must be *unstalled* quickly to stop dragging that aerial anchor of turbulent air and to regain some lift immediately.*

As soon as the stall is broken, the stick is brought smoothly back to normal gliding position because an unnecessary dive also would waste precious altitude. In general, the higher the nose position before the stall, the lower it will have to be in the recovery. As the glider accelerates, the nose should be raised smoothly so that best glide speed and its corresponding pitch attitude are attained at the same time.

Assuming the spoilers were open when the stall occurred, they should be closed to reduce drag and increase the effective area of the wing. The glider will regain best glide speed quicker and with less loss of altitude.

*An exception to this elevator usage is in a stall *very* close to the ground such as would occur after a bounced landing. Every effort should be made to touch down in a normal attitude rather than upon the nose of the glider, even though a hard landing results. Coming down on the nose is even harder.

Top rudder is used whenever one wing is lower than the other at the moment of stalling. In some gliders (not the training type) the use of aileron in a stall to pick up a low wing will have just the opposite effect. The down aileron stalls the low wing even further. At the stall, the rudder is still effective, and if fully applied will help to level the wings and to overcome any tendency of the glider to spin in the direction of the low wing. The instant the elevator unstalls the wing the ailerons will respond normally, and ailerons and rudder should then be used with normal coordination to level the glider.

The term "accelerated stall" means any stall in which the elevators are used to force the wing to a stalled angle of attack at an airspeed greater than the minimum stalling speed. In such a stall, recovery will result immediately when the stick is moved forward enough to reduce the angle of attack below the value for stalling. No altitude need be lost to regain speed since the stall is caused by misuse of the elevators rather than low speed. Accelerated stalls should not be performed above the maneuvering speed of the glider so as to avoid structural damage or failure.

The term "secondary stall" refers to a stall which occurs during a recovery from another (primary) stall. The cause obviously is that the pilot brought the stick back far enough to force the wing into a stalled angle of attack when completing the initial recovery. The wing could be stalled over and over again in this way, each stall occurring when the stick is brought back to the critical point where the wing stalls. Secondary stalls can easily "happen" when the pilot does not understand the relation between stick position and angle of attack of the wing.

SEQUENCE OF PRACTICE STALLS

For training purposes, five basic stalls are practiced in order. Each one simulates a low altitude situation that might give big trouble. The student should memorize these stalls and try to visualize their execution. This advance preparation will make the flight instruction easier and quicker.

Stalls are practiced upwind of the airport, and all turns are planned so as to stay within easy gliding range of the traffic pattern entry point. A 2500-foot tow provides ample altitude to run through the sequence more than once before getting down to 1500' AGL, which is the minimum legal altitude for the last three stalls. These are marginally "aerobatic" by FAA definition, or at least could be so. Begin with 90-degree clearing turns to right and left, checking below as well as horizontally. The five stalls are then performed in rapid succession, each one ending in a straight glide at best glide speed. This is the sequence:

1. A shallow stall straight ahead.
2. A turning stall with medium bank.
3. An accelerated stall from a steep bank in the opposite direction from 2 above.
4. A steep climbing stall straight ahead.
5. A steep climbing stall from a medium banked turn.

Throughout the sequence of stalls the student should visually clear the area, especially below. The stalls do not have to be so precise as to preclude looking for other aircraft.

The first stall simulates conditions during final approach when the pilot unintentionally raises the nose too high. This stall should be practiced with and without spoilers, and the nose should not be raised to an unrealistic degree considering the situation. The instant the nose cannot be held up with the elevator, recovery should be made.

The second stall simulates problems resulting from an incorrectly flown turn from the base leg to final approach. Bank should be 30 to 45 degrees, and the spoilers should be in various positions. The turn should not always be made in the same direction. The stall should be broken quickly, after which top aileron should be added to top rudder to produce a smooth and coordinated recovery to a straight glide.

The third stall simulates another problem in turning from the base leg to final approach. The assumption is that the pilot started the turn too late and then made a steep bank and tightened the turn with too much back stick, causing an accelerated stall. *Full* back stick will be required in most trainers. The spoilers should be used in varying degrees before stalling, as would be natural in flying the pattern. Recovery is simply a matter of closing the spoilers and moving the stick forward moderately to unstall the wing; then the glider is rolled level with normal coordination.

The fourth stall simulates conditions when the rope breaks in the steep part of an auto or winch tow. Spoilers are closed for this stall, and the pitch attitude is about 40 degrees nose up. It is assumed that the pilot was slow in reacting to the break and that a straight ahead stall results. Recovery requires the stick to be *all* the way forward until after the nose crosses the horizon, when it is moved slowly back. The recovery dive should be about the same degree below the horizon as the stall was above it. As speed increases the nose is brought up smoothly to a normal gliding attitude, being careful not to bring the stick back too far and thus provoke a secondary stall.

The fifth stall also simulates conditions after a ground launch rope break, but this stall occurs in a steep climbing turn, as if the pilot had started to turn back for a landing before lowering his nose. (The same attitude and stall could occur in a misjudged Chandelle, although no hazard would be involved since a Chandelle is always done above 1500' AGL, being decidedly aerobatic.) No spoilers are used for the climbing-turn stall.

SLOW FLIGHT

A part of the FAA flight test for a glider rating is a demonstration of flight at *minimum control speed* and at *minimum sink speed*. These are the terms used in the FAA flight test guide. Minimum control speed is not defined, and it is not an identifiable point on the glider performance curve. However, the glider is perfectly controllable slightly above stalling speed: plus two or three mph in smooth air, and plus five mph in moderately rough air. The minimum sink speed for any glider is given on the performance curve or in the manufacturer's flight instructions; in most training gliders it is six or seven mph above stalling. (See footnote on page 44.)

All that is required for the slow-flight test is straight flight and 20 to 30 degree banked turns at both required speeds. Criteria for performance are as follows:

1. Does the applicant look around?
2. Is he coordinated and smooth on the controls?
3. Does he control speed by controlling attitude?
4. Did he stall? (Buffeting is not stalling.)

In silky-smooth air the slow flight requirement is easy for a well-trained student. In turbulent air the minimum control speed portion can present a problem, and a few hints are in order. First, use a little judgment in choosing the speed, bearing in mind that flying a couple of miles an hour too fast is a less serious fault than stalling. Second, be careful not to bring the stick *all* the way back. (Recall that the elevators control angle of attack.) Third, control overbanking, staying *below* 30 degrees of bank. Fourth, roll in and out of banks slowly, giving careful attention to coordination. Fifth, be alert to relax back pressure on the stick just a trifle if a gust promotes an incipient stall; this will keep the glider "controllable" until the gust passes. The inspector will know it was a

gust. Sixth, look around by turning your head. The inspector can't see you rolling your eyeballs. Shift your attention continually between clearing the area, noting the attitude of the glider, and taking short peeks at the airspeed indicator and slip-skid ball or yaw string.

SPINS

At the present time a demonstration of spinning is not a part of the FAA flight test for glider pilots. This doesn't mean that spin training is not needed. The fact is that most gliders will spin if sufficiently provoked. There have been enough spin-type accidents to make abundantly clear the desirability of spin instruction for all glider pilots. In consequence, the Soaring Society of America has taken the strongest possible stand urging that all glider pilots receive spin instruction both on the ground and in the air, to the point of proficiency in spin entry and recovery. Precision spins are not suggested. Many schools refuse to solo a student until he has performed spins satisfactorily.

CAUTION: No pilot should undertake to teach himself spin technique or intentionally to spin a glider without having received dual instruction in spins.

Prevention of spin-type accidents is the best but not the only reason for spin instruction in gliders. Cloud flight in gliders not equipped for it or flown by pilots without instrument training quickly develops into a destructive high-speed spiral dive. Gliders can be trapped above the clouds in wave flying or drawn up into cumulo-nimbus against the pilot's will. The spin provides a safe means of descent through cloud so long as there is adequate clearance between cloud base and the ground (usually the case).

Spinning occurs when the glider is at or very near a stalled angle of attack and something causes one wing to become more stalled than the other, and so to fall. That something may be a wind gust, a skid, the way the glider is rigged, or the use of the controls. The angle of attack of the falling wing becomes greater, the wing stalls completely and its lift becomes negligible. Meanwhile, the angle of attack of the rising wing becomes less so it continues to lift effectively. The one-sided lift of the wings not only produces the spinning motion but allows the glider's nose to fall until the axis of the spin is vertically downward. This condition will continue as long as the inside wing remains stalled. When both wings are unstalled the

auto-rotation stops and the glider emerges from the spin in a nose-low attitude from which return to level flight is perfectly normal.

There is one more important point relating to spin theory. The location fore and aft of the center of gravity of the glider critically affects its spin characteristics. If the CG is too far back a flat spin will develop and recovery may be impossible.* When the CG is too far forward, the elevator control may be insufficient for slow flight or landing; spins will probably degenerate into high-speed spirals.

It is the pilot's responsibility to verify that the placard CG limitations are being complied with on *any* flight. If spins are planned, the pilot can go a little farther, and be sure the center of gravity is near the forward limit, which will assure rapid recovery.

The manufacturer's flight instructions should be checked before doing intentional spins in any glider, but especially in high-performance types. Some of the latter are restricted against intentional spins. If a stall in such a glider starts to fall off into an accidental spin, recovery should be initiated immediately and vigorously. The fully developed spin may rotate uncommonly fast, or require several turns to stop the spin, or have some other undesirable trait which would explain the prohibition of intentional spins.

GLIDER IN CLIMBING TURN
STICK BACK, ELEVATOR UP
ANGLE OF ATTACK NEAR 18 DEGREES
— ON THE EDGE OF A STALL

LEFT WING FALLS AND STALLS WORSE THAN RISING RIGHT WING. DIFFERENCE IN LIFT CAUSES ROTATION.

NOSE FALLS FOR LACK OF SUPPORT ON LEFT SIDE

PRACTICE SPINS

Spin instruction should be undertaken above 3500' AGL, which will allow altitude for several spins before reaching 1500' AGL, the minimum for aerobatics. The first step in the maneuver is to make two steep clearing turns, checking carefully for aircraft at lower levels.

*Before abandoning ship, open your seat belt and shift your weight as far forward as possible while applying recovery controls; a normal recovery may result. This sounds difficult-to-impossible, but it has happened more than once.

In a normally spinnable glider, entry is made from a shallow straight-ahead stall, without spoilers. Just before the nose drops, the stick is brought *straight back* (no ailerons) as far as it will go and full rudder is applied in the desired direction of spinning. Rotation will begin at once and will continue as long as the controls are held in that position.

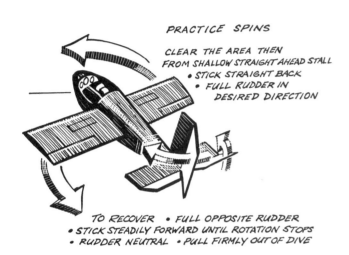

PRACTICE SPINS

CLEAR THE AREA THEN
FROM SHALLOW STRAIGHT AHEAD STALL
• STICK STRAIGHT BACK
• FULL RUDDER IN
  DESIRED DIRECTION

TO RECOVER • FULL OPPOSITE RUDDER
• STICK STEADILY FORWARD UNTIL ROTATION STOPS
• RUDDER NEUTRAL • PULL FIRMLY OUT OF DIVE

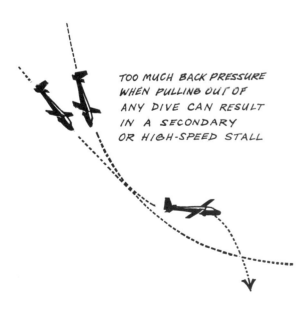

TOO MUCH BACK PRESSURE
WHEN PULLING OUT OF
ANY DIVE CAN RESULT
IN A SECONDARY
OR HIGH-SPEED STALL

To recover from the spin, the pilot applies full opposite rudder and moves the stick steadily forward until rotation stops. The rudder is then neutralized, and the pilot pulls out of the dive firmly to avoid unnecessary loss of altitude. The stick should not be brought back too far because of the possibility of an accelerated stall and another spin. However, the situation is no different from any other dive recovery.

Many two-place trainers, though spinnable, do not give a correct impression of normal spin behavior. They are reluctant spinners and overly speedy on the recovery. Spin training is far more valuable if taught in a glider with more representative spinning characteristics, such as the Schweizer 2-32. The extra cost for one rather short flight is more than compensated for by the increased instructional value.

One more fact about spins should be noted: many pilots thoroughly enjoy them.

ACCIDENTAL SPINS

Unintentional spinning should never occur with pilots who have been properly trained in stalls, spins and safe gliding habits.

To qualify the "never" statement, accidental spinning will not occur at low altitude when the pilot maintains the recommended pattern airspeed so that not even the worst atmospheric conditions near the ground can stall the glider's wing.

However, when circling in turbulent thermals at a safe altitude, momentary stalls and *incipient* spins are an occasional incident of soaring. With experience, the pilot will automatically recover from these incidents without even losing his position in the thermal.

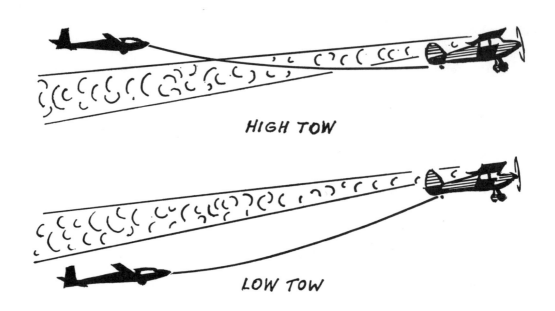

HIGH TOW

LOW TOW

PART I – GLIDING

5. AERO TOW

TOW POSITIONS

The two aero tow positions in common use are called *normal* or *high tow* and *low tow*. For the high tow position, the glider is five to ten feet above the towplane's wake, whereas for low tow the same distance is maintained below the wake. During aero tow the wake of the towplane is diverted downward, partly because the towplane is normally in a somewhat nose-high attitude, and partly because the wake is primarily caused by the downwash of the towplane's wing. As a result, the glider is about *level* with the towplane during high tow, and about thirty feet below during low tow.

Since the wing of a glider is much more powerful than the horizontal tail surface of the towplane, the glider can easily force the tug into a stall or dive. Therefore, the pilot of the glider must be alert to hold the chosen position within reasonable limits.

Both tow positions have their uses, and a well-trained pilot should be at home in either one, as well as feeling comfortable about moving from one to the other through the wake. At the present time the overwhelming majority of schools and clubs are using high tow in their day to day operations, and the increasing use of the adjective "normal" to describe it is fully justified. Low tow continues to be used in long cross-country tows, for a certain take-off situation and for landing while still on tow, as will be explained later.

HOLDING POSITION VERTICALLY

Three different methods of teaching how to hold position vertically are now being taught in the United States. All three have the same objective, and under favorable conditions work very well. Their differences lie in the reference points the student is instructed to keep in alignment so as to hold position. In unfavorable conditions the difference in reference-point techniques can be quite significant.

The first method is to control the glider so that the towplane remains at a certain position in relation to the horizon. The pilot dips into the wake to locate it, and then moves slightly above or below it. He then notes where the towplane appears to be with respect to the horizon and flies so as to keep it there. This system is much used in the Midwest, where flat terrain and a *usually* visible horizon favor it.

The second method is to maintain alignment between two points on the towplane, or to keep in view just so much of the top or bottom of its wing or fuselage, which amounts to the same thing. Thus the towplane, its wake and the glider keep a constant relationship independent of a possibly obscure horizon line. Small changes in the pitch attitude of the towplane require larger changes in the vertical position of the glider because of the geometry of the relationship. In strong thermal turbulence or when towing through the rotor of a wave system, the towplane's pitching tends to make the glider pilot use exaggerated and sometimes out-of-phase corrections. Slack in the line becomes a problem, and rope breaks occur more often than need be.

The third, and preferred, technique is to keep the towplane in a fixed position on the glider's windshield. This position on the windshield is where the towplane appears after the right relationship to the wake has been established, as was done with the other two methods. In high tow, the towplane appears near the bottom of the windshield, and in low tow near the top. The exact location depends on the pilot's seating position and the resulting eye level. When the towplane appears to move up or down from the correct point on the windshield, the pilot smoothly applies pressure on the ele-

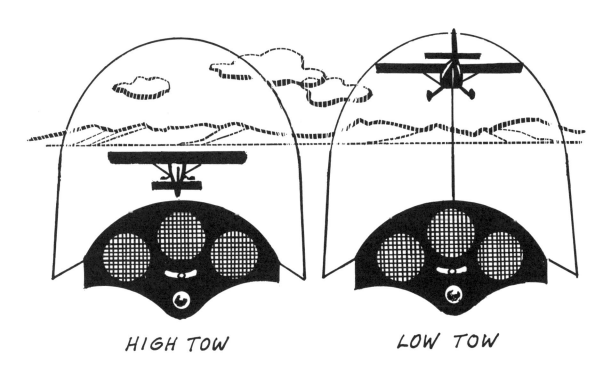

HIGH TOW   LOW TOW

TO HOLD POSITION VERTICALLY — KEEP
TOWPLANE IN POSITION ON GLIDER'S WINDSHIELD

vator to put it back in place, refraining from correcting further because (by some other criterion) the tug looks out of position. In effect, the glider pilot aligns two points *in the glider* upon the towplane, his own eyes and an area on the plexiglas, thus *aiming* the glider at the towplane. The geometry of this system of holding position results in smaller corrections which diminish further as the desired relationship of towplane and glider is neared. In rough air, if the towplane shoots up or down a substantial amount, as it often does, the glider pilot changes the glider's pitch attitude only enough to regain his aim. Changes in the pitch attitude of the towplane or the disappearance of the horizon have no effect on this technique.

One might argue that a *skilled* pilot uses a fourth concept of following on tow: that is, he knows where he wants to be in relationship to the towplane, and just stays there. This inherent-sense method is very hard to teach beginners as they neither recognize displacements of position without some guide nor know how to get back in position without over-correcting and setting up wild oscillations. What is more, in really rough air even the expert pilot might prefer the ease of the aiming concept.

During aero tow, some gliders (including trainers) tend to zoom unless restrained by constant forward pressure on the stick. This occurs in part because the speed during tow is greater than the speed for which the glider is rigged or trimmed. Another factor is the location of the tow hook at the bottom of the glider's fuselage. Factors which mitigate this condition in other gliders are a forward and higher position of the towhook, adequate trimming devices, and relatively neutral pitch stability designed into the glider.

HOLDING POSITION LATERALLY

Aero Tow can be looked upon as a simplified kind of formation flying. A close formation, considered as a unit, seems to fly as a single aircraft. The wing men keep their wings parallel to the leader's wings and edge in and out with rudder and fore and aft with power changes. A glider has the tow rope to control the fore and aft relationship. The wings are kept parallel to the towplane's wings, and the glider cannot move out of position sideways so long as no rudder pressure is applied.

If the glider *does* move out to one side of the towplane, the glider pilot has to decide whether he is holding a wing down (most probable), pushing on a rudder pedal without realizing it, or both. Leveling the glider's wings with those of the towplane and neutralizing the rudder will automatically allow the glider to slide over straight behind the tug; there is no force acting to hold it out to the side.

When the glider pilot wishes to move out of line to one side of the tug, this can be done by banking relative to the towplane or by applying rudder while keeping the wings parallel to the tug's. The latter method is far easier to manage without overdoing it. When a bank is used to move *far* out to the side (as when signaling the tow pilot), the angle of bank should be very slight.

During aero tow, coordination of aileron and rudder to balance out adverse yaw is generally normal. An exception is when the pilot yaws the glider intentionally to increase drag; this maneuver is like a forward slip and is accomplished with opposite stick and rudder.

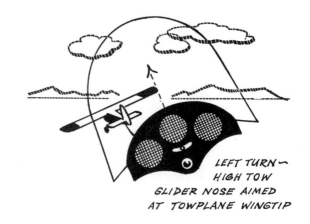

LEFT TURN—
HIGH TOW
GLIDER NOSE AIMED
AT TOWPLANE WINGTIP

When the towplane and glider bank into a turn simultaneously, the glider will turn slightly inside the towplane. This lateral displacement is too small to affect safety. Some instructors prefer a more elegant style, and teach the student to delay banking two or three seconds, and then to keep the glider aimed at the outside wing-tip of the towplane while the turn is in progress. This technique, which tends to keep the glider turning on the perimeter of the same circle as the towplane, is an unnecessary refinement, but still a refinement.

SLACK IN THE TOWLINE

A glider normally follows the towplane at a rearward distance determined by the length of the rope. However, a change in the speed of either aircraft that allows them to come closer will create a slack line. When speeds are substantially different, a great loop can develop that could ensnare the glider or foul its controls. A moment later when the speed difference reverses, the line comes tight with a snap, and the glider may be damaged or the rope may break. In the latter case, the part of the rope still attached to the glider may fly back and become entangled in the controls.

Offhand, one might think that a glider on tow could not accelerate above the speed of its tug and thus overtake it. Not so. There are several ways for the glider to acquire extra speed. Here are a few:

1. When the tug initiates a turn and the glider pilot is slow in banking with it, the glider will turn outside the towplane, on a longer radius, and so go both farther and faster. No one who has, in his youth, played crack-the-whip on skates will fail to understand this speed difference.

2. When the glider pilot climbs above the normal tow position, the fixed length of the towline causes the glider to move forward as well as up, gaining speed

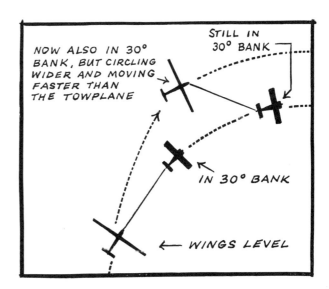

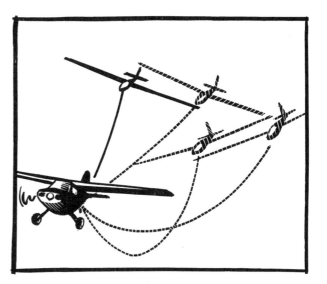

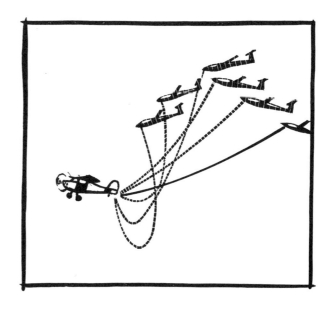

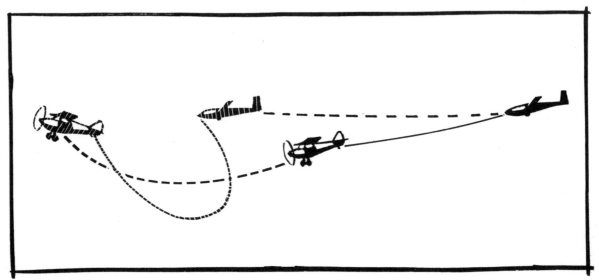

as it goes. If this motion is continued the glider can reach a point almost above the tug. Having gained speed by pulling up, the glider can gain even more by diving down toward the towplane. The glider's aerodynamic cleanness makes this possible.

3. If the glider banks and moves rapidly to the side, the fixed length of the rope will cause it to move forward relative to the towplane, accelerating as it does so. If the pilot then *turns back* toward the correct position, the extra speed will cause a slack towline. This explains why a sideways error of position should be corrected by merely leveling the glider's wings rather than banking relative to the towplane's wings.

4. The towplane may dip down, accelerating both aircraft, and then pull up again, slowing itself but not the glider. Either tow-pilot error or vertical air currents can cause the dip.

5. In a let-down, the glider may over-run the towplane because of the glider's lesser drag. To combat this problem, the glider pilot has only to increase the drag of his craft, either by opening spoilers, yawing, or by lowering the wheel if the glider has retractable gear.

When the glider is in an accelerating situation the pilot can still prevent a slack line by yawing the glider, i.e., by crossing controls to create drag. As the glider turns back toward the towplane this extra drag will slow the glider, keeping the line taut. Spoilers may also be used for the same purpose, but the yaw is favored because it is quicker than unlocking and deploying the spoilers and may be controlled with greater nicety.

Should the pilot see slack actually appearing in the towline, he should take *immediate* corrective action. A sharp yaw can quickly stop the development of a towline loop. The yaw

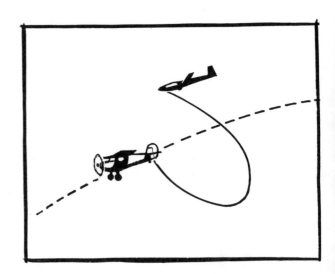

should be discontinued the instant the sag in the line *stops increasing;* this condition indicates that the two aircraft are once again going the same speed. Now the problem is to remove the existing slack without breaking the line.

Before discussing the removal of slack, let's assume that a gross error has been made and that a large loop of towline is streaming back alongside, above, or below the glider. The pilot's first thought should be to stay away from that big loop to avoid entanglement. If the loop is on the left, move right; if it is above the glider, move down, and so on. *GET AWAY FROM IT!* Doing so will not only avoid dan-

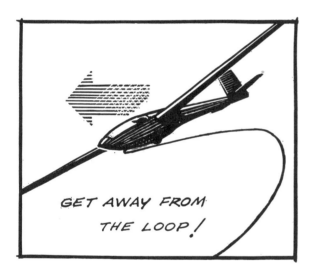

GET AWAY FROM THE LOOP!

ger but will take some of the slack out of the line. Should the glider pilot wish to release, he should first move to a position where he is certain the freed towline will stay clear of the glider. By then there will probably be no necessity to release.

When the slack in the towline has stopped increasing, the problem is to draw the line straight, but *slowly,* so as to preclude snapping the towline. While the line is slack the towplane has no tow load and can thus accelerate rapidly. For this reason the loop in the line disappears with increasing swiftness. The glider pilot must try to equalize the speeds

of tug and glider just before the rope draws up tight. This requires smoothly nosing the glider down to gain speed. While this is going on, the glider's wings should be kept parallel to those of the towplane. After the rope comes taut the glider is allowed to swing in behind the towplane in a normal manner.

When a slack line appears the pilot can further reduce stress on the rope (when it tightens again) by taking a position away from the longitudinal axis of the towplane in the most convenient direction. As the line tightens the oblique pull on the nose of the glider and the tail of the towplane causes both craft to pivot slightly, and this yielding serves to minimize the shock.

FLYING THROUGH THE WAKE

The term "Wake" means the total disturbance in the air behind the towplane. Two elements make up the wake: the downwash of the wing, including the vortices from the wingtips, and the slipstream of the propeller. The only one that has a significant effect on the flight of the glider is the downwash of the wing. The towplane's wing works just like the glider's, forcing down the air and so supporting the aircraft. The air behind the towplane for many hundreds of feet has a considerable downward motion. When the glider's wing is in this de-

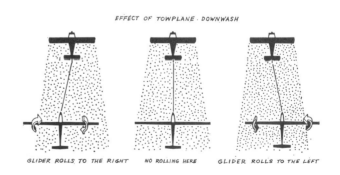

EFFECT OF TOWPLANE DOWNWASH

GLIDER ROLLS TO THE RIGHT   NO ROLLING HERE   GLIDER ROLLS TO THE LEFT

scending air the effect is to decrease its angle of attack and lift.

When the glider is laterally centered behind

the towplane, both wings are equally affected; the principal area of each wing is in the downwash, and equal spans at each tip project out into undisturbed air beyond the wake. There is no rolling force imparted to the glider. However, when the glider is slightly off center to the right, for example, the right wing would extend farther into the undisturbed air and the left wing would be more within the downwash. The effect would be the same as if the pilot had moved the stick to the left. The opposite would occur if the glider were on the left side of the tug's centerline. The rolling of the glider will always be toward the extended centerline of the towplane. The wingtip vortex works in the same direction as the downwash and generally cannot be detected by the glider pilot as a force separate from it.

The second component of the wake is the propeller slipstream. At one time this was blamed for "a severe spiral turbulence." The glider was supposed to bank violently in a clockwise direction, the direction of rotation of the propeller, and to shoot off to the right.

One day, some unremembered pilot noticed that there was no banking tendency right at the point where it should have been worst, i.e., when the two fuselages were in exact alignment. Investigating further, he discovered that when the glider was displaced slightly to the right, the banking force was *against* the direction of propeller rotation. At this point the severe spiral turbulence joined the airpocket and many other legends of the air.

This is not to say that the propwash has no effect on the glider. Indeed it does. It produces a mild shaking of the glider and a drumming of its fabric, if it has any. The vibration of the drumming is quite clearly related to the propeller's rotation. The effect of this pulsation is perfectly harmless and does not affect the flight of the glider.

When the glider pilot wishes to move from normal tow to low tow, or vice versa, he should align the glider accurately behind the tug and then move smoothly but firmly through the wake. This is the easiest route, but by no means the only way. The glider's aileron power is ample to control the rolling force anywhere in the wake if promptly and decisively applied. When the glider moves through to the other side of the wake in a banked attitude the forces are reversed, tending to roll the glider level again. Much fun may be had examining the effects of the downwash on the glider by trying to stay in a constant attitude in various parts of the wake. The game will increase the pilot's understanding of the dimensions and the character of the wake. If things get out of hand, it is only necessary to move out of the wake and think out what was done wrong before trying again.

FLYING AROUND THE WAKE

Demonstrating the ability to fly around the towplane's wake is part of the FAA flight test. This maneuver is performed entirely in the undisturbed air surrounding the wake, and in an earlier era may have been the route from high tow to low tow and back for the soaring chicken.

In performing this maneuver the only difficulty the pilot may run into is a tendency to develop a slack line when descending to the level of low tow. This may be overcome either (1) by descending very slowly, or (2) by yawing to increase the glider's drag, or (3) by opening the spoilers partly. Take your choice; they all work.

Here are six steps for performing this requirement for the flight test in the easiest possible way, flying a 2-place trainer. The glider's wings are kept parallel with those of the towplane and motion sideways accomplished with rudder alone.

1. Use rudder to slide out beyond the towplane's wingtip.

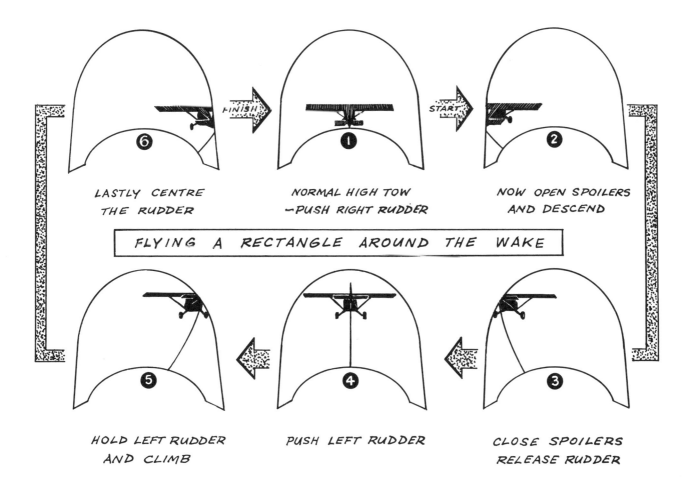

LASTLY CENTRE
THE RUDDER

NORMAL HIGH TOW
—PUSH RIGHT RUDDER

NOW OPEN SPOILERS
AND DESCEND

FLYING A RECTANGLE AROUND THE WAKE

HOLD LEFT RUDDER
AND CLIMB

PUSH LEFT RUDDER

CLOSE SPOILERS
RELEASE RUDDER

2. Holding the rudder, open the spoilers half way and descend.

3. Close the spoilers and release the rudder to move back toward the center.

4. Apply opposite rudder to move out to the opposite side.

5. Holding the rudder, climb to the high-tow level.

6. *Slowly* release the rudder to align the glider behind the towplane without overshooting.

Some high-performance gliders, the 2-32 among them, will need a slight amount of bank to move out beyond the towplane's wingtip.

After the flight test this maneuver will probably never be done again, since it is so much easier and quicker to move to the other tow position directly.

SIGNALING THE TOWPLANE

Radio offers the best means of communication between the pilots of the towplane and glider. In the absence of this costly convenience, the glider pilot can indicate a desire for a right turn by pulling the tug's tail to the left, and vice versa. This has the effect of aiming the tug where the glider pilot wants to go unless the tow pilot opposes the turn.

Pre-arrangement between pilots is desirable to avoid misunderstanding. With no prior agreement, the towplane pilot might wonder if the glider was just out of position, practicing a box around the wake, or giving a signal. Or his thoughts might simply be elsewhere.

Appendix B illustrates all the Standard American Soaring Signals both on the ground and in the air.

RELEASE POINT
GLIDER MAKES
CLIMBING TURN
TO THE
RIGHT

TOWPLANE MAKES
DESCENDING
TURN TO THE
LEFT

RELEASE FROM TOW

Release is done with the line under its usual tension so the tow pilot will feel the release. When the glider pilot *sees* the rope snap forward he climbs to the right, away from the trailing tow rope.

The towpilot, on feeling the release, must verify it visually before changing course. When he is certain, he makes a descending turn to the left, eliminating any possibility of interference with the glider.

Any variation from the above procedure, as for example when towing into ridge or wave lift, should be by explicit pre-arrangement between the pilots or by written rule of the operator of the soaring site.

AERO TOW TAKE-OFF

When a student has become competent at aero tow aloft he is ready for take-off instruction. By this time he will have made a number of flights and will understand the signals and routine of take-off. Let's assume that the glider is just starting to move forward. The stick should be held back (in a trainer) to raise the nose skid off the ground as quickly as possible, and then moved forward as necessary to keep the glider in a level pitch attitude while accelerating. When the wing runner lets go, the

pilot must keep the wings level with the ailerons and the fuselage lined up with the rudder. This is not the normal coordination of free flight, as the glider is rolling, not flying. Full and prompt use of both controls will be needed until speed picks up.

When the airspeed is well above stalling, around 40 mph in a trainer, and the glider feels buoyant and ready to fly in a level attitude, it should be lifted cleanly off the ground and held at an altitude of three to six feet. Coordination is now normal. Great care should be used in keeping low until the towplane is airborne, since the glider could pull the tug's tail up, preventing it from taking off or forcing it back to the ground thereafter. This would be no occasion for mirth. The glider should be no higher than the upper part of the tug's fuselage.

WRONG

RIGHT

TAKING OFF — STAY LOW, NEAR SAME LEVEL AS TOWPLANE

In advance of take-off, an emergency release point should be selected which would leave the pilot plenty of room to land straight ahead using full spoilers, and brakes after touching down. Should there be any indication of towplane feebleness or other difficulty, the glider pilot releases. This is important (lumping all the unfavorable factors together) when flying a heavy 2-place glider from a high altitude field on a hot calm day, while being towed by a tug of moderate power. The high density altitude of such conditions further reduces the towplane's power, while requiring a higher ground speed before either aircraft can fly.

After taking off under the above severe conditions, the glider pilot may see that the tug's ability to clear an obstacle is marginal. He can help the situation by staying close to the ground until the towplane has climbed to the position used in low tow. The glider then climbs maintaining this relationship until the tug clears the obstacle, after which he climbs to the high tow position in time to clear the obstacle also. The effect of this maneuver is that the towplane does not have to lift the glider up to high tow position until it clears the obstacle and can use this energy for its own climb. *Great* care must be used by the glider pilot to avoid a too-low position which would pull the tug's tail down causing it to stall.

When the glider pilot's visibility is briefly obscured by dust from the towplane, as can happen on a dirt field, he concentrates on keeping the wings level, looking down, to the side, or perhaps at a cloud ahead of the tug. The pull of the towrope will keep the glider straight if the wings are kept level. The dust will clear in a few seconds.

In a cross-wind take-off, the chief problem is directional control. The wing runner should be instructed to run the upwind wingtip, and to hold it a little lower than the other one. He must not pull the wingtip either way during his run. The pilot holds *full* rudder on the downwind side as the glider begins to roll. When the runner releases the wingtip, the pilot continues to hold it slightly low to prevent the wind from getting under it, swerving the glider. Meanwhile he will be holding rudder on the downwind side as needed to keep the glider lined up with the runway and the towplane. When airborne, the rudder should be released and the glider flown with normal coordination. A crabbing heading into the wind should be held to

make it easier for the towpilot to stay lined up with the runway. After a few seconds the towplane will be airborne, and its pilot will be responsible for crabbing and establishing direction for both craft. The glider pilot merely brings his wings parallel to the tug's, and drifts into normal aero tow position. From this point on, normal aero tow principles prevail.

Students often ask if there is a maximum cross-wind velocity at which the glider can still be safely taken off. There is, of course, but it is hard to pin down because of the many variables involved, e.g., the angle of the cross-wind, the controllability of the glider, the acceleration of the towplane and the skill of the glider pilot. Sometimes high-performance sailplanes have to stay on the ground when school trainers are having little difficulty. In this matter, pilot judgment comes with experience, best acquired gradually. In a strong cross-wind, be ready to release at the first sign of loss of control.

AERO TOW EMERGENCY PROCEDURES

The vast majority of aero tows are entirely without incident. As a result, too many pilots forget that once in a while the rope breaks, the release doesn't release, or the tug's engine fails. If the pilot has a proper emergency plan in mind before each take-off, the "emergencies" will be mere routine incidents of soaring.

When the rope breaks, the glider pilot must decide what to do with the dangling rope and what course to take with the glider. Regarding the former, the rope must be kept free of trees, fence, etc., and must not be dropped where it could do damage. It may be dropped on the runway or some other safe area, or the pilot may land with it still dangling if there is sufficient altitude and runway for a safe high approach.

The course to take with the glider depends on its altitude and airspeed, on the wind, and on conditions of the local terrain. At low alti-

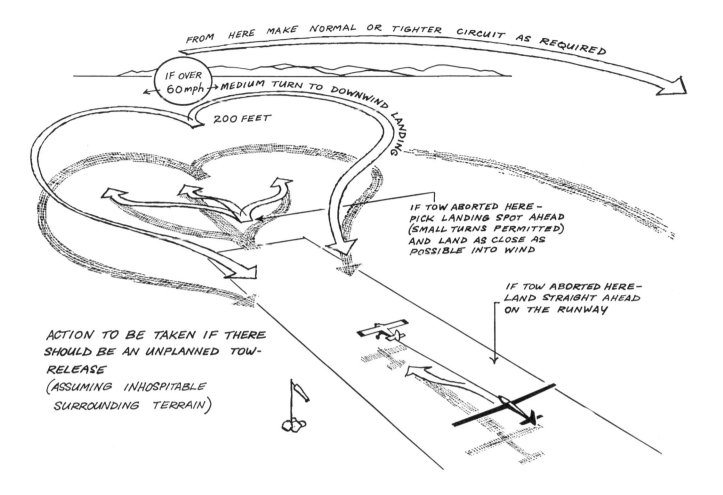

FROM HERE MAKE NORMAL OR TIGHTER CIRCUIT AS REQUIRED

IF OVER 60 mph → MEDIUM TURN TO DOWNWIND LANDING

200 FEET

IF TOW ABORTED HERE — PICK LANDING SPOT AHEAD (SMALL TURNS PERMITTED) AND LAND AS CLOSE AS POSSIBLE INTO WIND

IF TOW ABORTED HERE — LAND STRAIGHT AHEAD ON THE RUNWAY

ACTION TO BE TAKEN IF THERE SHOULD BE AN UNPLANNED TOW-RELEASE (ASSUMING INHOSPITABLE SURROUNDING TERRAIN)

tude and slow speed, below 200' AGL and at less than 60 mph, a small turn may be possible in order to reach a good landing spot. If higher and *faster* (speed is far more important) than the stated minimums, the pilot can make a 180 degree turn and land downwind, though a strong wind would make this a poor decision. In a two-place trainer a 180 degree turn could be entered at 63 mph and completed at 48 mph (which is 50% over stalling speed) without losing *any* altitude. A medium bank is recommended for this maneuver; a shallow bank is too slow and wastes altitude, and a steeply-banked turn, with higher sink rate, does likewise. Besides, a steep turn in the disturbed air close to the ground is most unwise.

The glider pilot can usually feel a loss of power or towplane engine failure. When this happens he *must* release the towrope at once and follow his plan for a rope break. The tow-plane pilot, relieved of his tow, has a much better chance of solving his problem. If there is enough runway ahead he will land and clear to the left, leaving room for the glider to land on the right side. Should the glider pilot fail to notice a loss of power, the towplane pilot will rock his wings, which is the signal for *mandatory* release.

Regarding failure of the glider towhook to release, which is rather unlikely if the pilot tested it before take-off, the procedure is simple. The pilot of the glider moves well out to the side to attract the towpilot's attention, and then rocks his wings. The towplane pilot will then fly over the field above 2000' AGL and release the tow rope from his end. The glider pilot then proceeds with a higher than usual approach to avoid snagging the tow rope.

If the towpilot also cannot release (improbability raised to the Nth power), he will signal the fact to the glider pilot by fanning his rudder. Towplane and glider will now land together, still connected by the tow rope. This may sound difficult but in fact is not, and practicing it is good fun until the novelty wears off. Here is how it is done. The glider pilot moves into low tow position and opens his spoilers partially to avoid over-running the tug during the let-down. The towplane pilot plans a long and shallow power approach that will clear the boundary obstacles with enough margin (about 50 feet) for the glider to get over safely. The glider lands first, being lower, and zips along on its wheel while the towplane descends the last 30 feet and lands. During this speedy rollout the glider pilot should close the spoilers and refrain from putting down the nose skid or applying wheel brake. Should he do so, the towplane could be stalled out and slammed down hard, with possible damaging effect.

TOW ROPES AND RELEASES

Selection and preparation of tow ropes for aero tow or ground launch is not the responsibility of the student pilot. If it ever should become his problem, he is commended to the American Soaring Handbook, Chapter 8, which discusses the subject fully.

The FAA written test for a glider rating has questions on the subject, and in this instance a little knowledge is *not* a "dangerous thing." First, there is no FAA regulation with respect to towrope length for aero tow. Nevertheless, the electronic test grader is firmly of the opinion that the rope should be 200 feet long. The fact is, longer ropes are uneconomic and shorter ones are a little more difficult for the glider pilot in rough air. On sandy fields, short ropes will allow the propwash to sandblast the glider. An advantage of a short rope, about 75 to 100 feet long, is that it may make possible an aero retrieve out of a small pasture or farm field, a fact worth remembering.

Regarding tow rope breaking strength, the FAA quite properly has a regulation. If the tow rope is too weak, there is danger of an untimely break; if too strong it could transmit damaging loads to the glider in a variety of unhappy circumstances. A rope that breaks *when it should* offers a protection similar to that of a fuse in an electrical circuit. Hark well: the required breaking strength of the rope must be over 80% and less than 200% of the gross weight of the glider being towed.

When stronger rope or steel cable is used, as is often the case in winch or auto launching, there must be a weak link at the glider end of the line. The breaking strength of the weak link must be the same as is required for plain tow ropes without weak links.

Regarding the release mechanism (towhook), the applicant for a license should be aware that both the design and the installation on towplane and glider are subject to FAA approval.

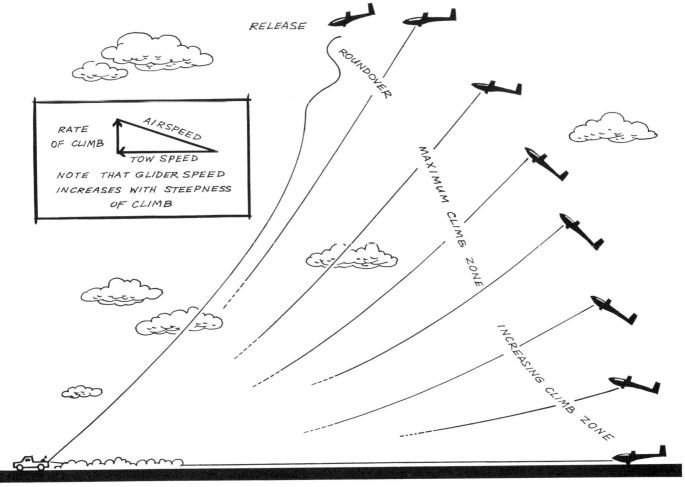

RATE OF CLIMB

AIRSPEED

TOW SPEED

NOTE THAT GLIDER SPEED INCREASES WITH STEEPNESS OF CLIMB

RELEASE

ROUNDOVER

MAXIMUM CLIMB ZONE

INCREASING CLIMB ZONE

STAGES OF AUTO TOW

PART I – GLIDING

6. GROUND LAUNCH

GENERAL INFORMATION

From the glider pilot's point of view there is no important difference between the techniques of winch launch and auto tow. When **steel cable is used** (complete with weak link, as previously explained) a small **parachute** is incorporated near the glider to keep the cable from tying itself in knots when released. As in aero tow, both ends of the line must be quickly releasable. (A winch uses a guillotine to cut the cable.) A tow car should have an observer to watch the glider and relay signals to the driver. At the glider, there should be an assistant to hook up the line, signal to the tow-car and to run the wing.

Signals are *best* given by radio, but most schools and clubs are not so luxuriously equipped. The customary aero tow signal for take-off (rudder wagging) often cannot be seen from the end of a long line, so special signals may have to be arranged. Here is *one* system that has worked well:

1. Hold one wing on the ground until the car crew has hooked up.
2. Signal for the car to take up slack by raising and lowering the wing as far as possible in a continuous pumping motion until the slack is all out.
3. Hold the glider's wings level when the pilot is ready for take-off.
4. If not ready, signify "Hold" by lowering the wingtip to the ground.
5. In flight, rocking the wings is the standard signal for an increase of 5 mph in the towing speed.
6. Fishtailing the glider with the rudder is the standard signal for a reduction of 5 mph.

Before signaling for a further speed change, allow the driver a few seconds to take action on the first signal.

TOW SPEED CONSIDERATIONS

Before beginning a tow, the pilot must advise the driver or winch operator what speed to use. (This is part of the FAA flight test.) To arrive at this figure the pilot starts with the placard maximum speed for ground launch and makes four deductions from it in line with his best judgment of existing conditions as follows: (1) surface wind velocity, (2) about 10 mph for the glider's increase in speed in a climb, (3) an allowance for the wind velocity gra-

dient, and (4) a further safety factor to stay comfortably below the maximum allowable speed. Here is an example of this calculation for the first flight of the day in a Schweizer 2-33 when the surface wind is 5 mph.

Auto tow red line	69 mph
Less surface wind	64 mph
Less effect of climbing	54 mph
Less est. wind gradient	50 mph
Less safety factor	45 mph

The pilot knows he is safely above the 32 mph stalling speed so advises the driver to go 45 mph, but cautions the observer to stay alert for speed signals. After the first tow he will know better what conditions call for. (Often a 5 mph speed reduction is prearranged when the glider reaches maximum angle of climb.)

TAKE-OFF

The tow rope should be laid out obliquely to the line of take-off so that the glider will be 100 to 200 feet to one side (the down-wind side if there is a cross-wind) of the intended line of flight. The tow rope is not connected to the glider until the pilot is fully ready to go, the canopy closed and the checklist completed except for "Connect cable, test release, reconnect." The glider must be aimed 15 to 20 degrees away from the towline and toward the extended axis of the take-off, and must be held that way through the ground run. This tactic will prevent the glider from running over the line or becoming entangled in it if the towcar should stall or the line should break. Tow cars usually make the entire run in second gear, both to avoid a shift bobble and for plenty of power. When the glider is airborne, it should be lined up with the direction of tow, or in a crosswind, slightly upwind of it so the towline will fall on the runway after release. The ground run, crosswind corrections, and the lift-off are similar to those for aero tow, but easier for the glider pilot because of the faster acceleration.

Schweizer 2-32 — photo by George Uveges

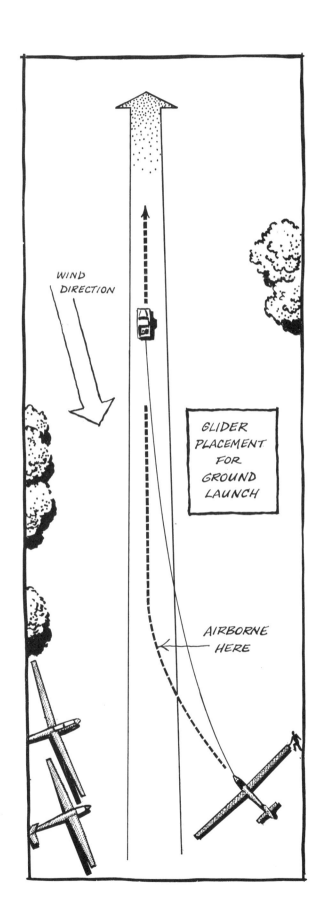

WIND
DIRECTION

GLIDER
PLACEMENT
FOR
GROUND
LAUNCH

AIRBORNE
HERE

THE INITIAL CLIMB

The pilot's chief concern in the early part of the climb is that his pitch attitude is moderate until some altitude is gained and airspeed is up to normal. Should the rope break or the tow car stall, a safe landing should always be possible. As usual, speed is more important in this regard than altitude. After the wheel leaves the ground there should be a *brief* period of acceleration without climb. Then the nose of the glider is slowly, smoothly and continuously raised until the maximum pitch angle is attained. Since the nose of the glider soon hides the horizon ahead, the pilot must judge the pitch attitude by the angle of the wingtip against the horizon at the side. As a rough guide to pulling up, the pitch angle should not exceed 15 degrees at 50 feet *indicated* altitude, 30 degrees at 100 feet and 45 degrees (the maximum) at 200 feet. The rate of climb is so rapid that the altimeter will be behind the actual altitude about 50 feet when it indicates 50 feet above the runway, increasing to as much as 150 feet behind in the steepest part of the climb. Actually, in the event of a rope break, the critical factor is airspeed. If this is up to normal (around 55 mph indicated) when the rope breaks, and the stick is slammed fully forward instantly at the crack of the breaking line, the glider will come to a normal gliding attitude while still above best glide speed. No crisis. Next, pull the release a couple of times to drop the end of the line attached to the glider, and land following the prearranged plan, which is dependent on available altitude and local geography.

THE STEEP CLIMB

A pilot is taught that raising the nose of his craft will slow it down. In a ground launch, the opposite is true. The explanation is quite simple. In level flight the glider's speed is the same as the winch or tow car speed. When climbing, the horizontal speed is unchanged, but a vertical component of motion has been added. The resultant speed of the glider therefore increases in proportion to the steepness of the climb.

A second factor that increases airspeed above that of the tow car is the wind velocity gradient; a third is possible wind gusts. These factors can lead a careless pilot to exceed the placard maximum speed for ground launch. This is a speed limit that deserves the utmost respect. It should be noted that stresses from these causes are imposed on the glider, but the tow cable prevents the pilot from feeling them as he does the maneuvering and gust loads of free flight. The pilot has no warning of high stresses other than the indicated airspeed.

In view of the potential danger from unexpected wind gusts, a pilot is unwise to allow the airspeed to get close to the maximum permissible. If it does, he must *immediately* decrease the angle of climb. Only then, with the airspeed reduced, should he "fishtail" for a lower tow speed. When the signal has produced the desired results the pilot can again steepen his climb.

When the glider is low and too slow, the pilot's action depends upon *how* slow. If within ten mph of stalling speed, it is wise to maintain a conservative angle of climb and to rock the wings for more speed. If at a safe altitude, the pilot may signal for more speed and at the same time pull up to a steeper climb angle, thus increasing the speed enough for a safe recovery if the rope should break.

ROUNDOVER AND RELEASE

As the glider nears the top of its climb the rate of climb will diminish, as will the pitch attitude and airspeed. The glider should then be levelled off to reduce the tension on the towhook and the release pulled a couple of times to be sure it has functioned. If there is any doubt about the release, the pilot glides straight ahead past the winch or tow car, where

the backward pull of the cable will operate the automatic release. If two-way radio is in use, the ground crew confirms the release.

TOW HOOK LOCATION

The tow hook may be located near the nose of the glider, or anywhere along the lower part of the fuselage as far back as the main wheel. Some gliders even have two hooks. The forward position is primarily for aero tow and the rear position for ground launch. Hook position significantly affects the way the glider handles and the loads imposed upon it.

When a nose hook is used for ground launch, the pull is partly downward on the nose of the glider, far ahead of the center of lift of the wing. To keep the wing at a high angle of attack against this pull requires a balancing downward force on the tail. This is provided by the up elevator. The wing must support the weight of the glider *plus* the added downward forces on the nose and tail. Thus the stress on the wing is greater the farther forward the hook is located. Stick loads are also heavier, and the angle of climb and altitude gained will be less with a far forward location of the hook.

Another effect of the nose hook can be a pitch oscillation called *porpoising*. If the extreme up elevator causes the horizontal tail surfaces to stall and become ineffective, the nose

"PORPOISING" ON AUTO OR WINCH TOW

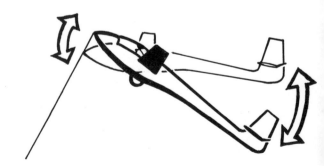

THE CURE —MOVE STICK FORWARD UNTIL PORPOISING STOPS

will be pulled downward by the cable. Almost immediately the tail becomes unstalled and the nose starts back up again. The porpoising, unless checked, will become greater and will probably cause a rope break. The corrective action is to relax the back pressure on the stick and settle for a slightly shallower angle of climb.

The rearward location of the towhook, called a belly hook or a CG hook, is well suited to ground launch. In the steep part of the climb, the line of the tow rope, extended, would pass through or slightly ahead of the center of gravity of the glider. (In a few instances, behind the CG.) There is little or no downward pull on the nose. Total wingloading and stick pressures are lower, and once the desired climb is established very little use of the elevator is needed to maintain it. A disadvantage is the fact that the pilot can easily climb too steeply. Paradoxically, this would not bring about a stall in view of the fact that the glider's motion is steeply upward. Instead, the airspeed would shoot up, increasing the wing loading to a dangerous degree and would probably break the towrope. Here is where the weak link is a lifesaver.

In actual practice, the 45 degree climb which is normal for a ground launch using a CG hook is pretty exciting for a pilot who has been conditioned to the danger of a stall when the nose is held only slightly above the horizon. It feels like the initial climb on a roller coaster. In consequence, pilots don't often pull up too steeply. Those who have been taught to take the airspeed indication very seriously *never* climb too steeply.

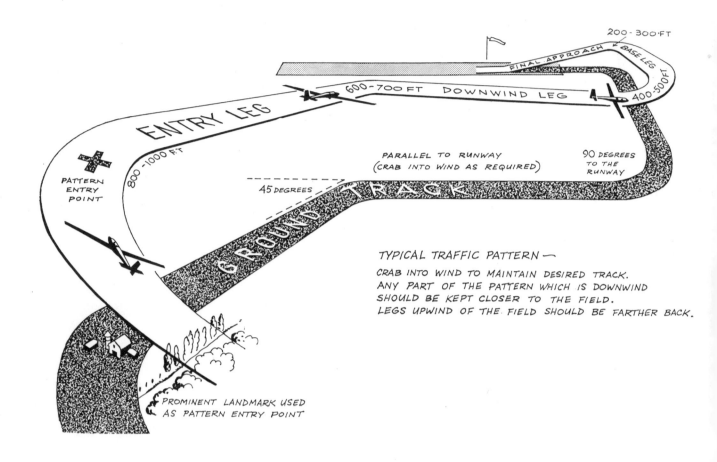

200-300·FT

FINAL APPROACH

BASE LEG

600-700 FT   DOWNWIND LEG

400-500 FT

ENTRY LEG

800-1000 FT

PARALLEL TO RUNWAY
(CRAB INTO WIND AS REQUIRED)

90 DEGREES
TO THE
RUNWAY

PATTERN
ENTRY
POINT

45 DEGREES

GROUND TRACK

TYPICAL TRAFFIC PATTERN —

CRAB INTO WIND TO MAINTAIN DESIRED TRACK.
ANY PART OF THE PATTERN WHICH IS DOWNWIND
SHOULD BE KEPT CLOSER TO THE FIELD.
LEGS UPWIND OF THE FIELD SHOULD BE FARTHER BACK.

PROMINENT LANDMARK USED
AS PATTERN ENTRY POINT

PART I – GLIDING

7. THE TRAFFIC PATTERN

PURPOSE AND RULES

The purpose of a traffic pattern is to ensure an approach with proper spacing from other traffic and a safe landing at a predetermined spot on the landing area. When all gliders fly the same pattern, each pilot knows where to look for the others and can more easily space himself away from them. The most used pattern requires the pilot to fly step by step through a familiar succession of four turning points and four straight legs. At each turning point he knows how high he should be and what the apparent downward angle should be from his position to the landing spot. The pilot also has learned how to adjust his pattern, so that when the final approach is established, landing close to the mark becomes easy and almost inevitable. This certainty of position throughout the traffic pattern to the point of landing is essential in an aircraft without the power to pull up and go around for a second try.

Conditions at different airports necessitate many variations from the standard pattern to be discussed here. All patterns have in common a fixed Entry Point at a stated altitude above some landmark, and a Base Leg at 90 degrees to the final approach. The intermediate legs may vary to suit local needs. A pattern is required for each direction of landing, and sometimes two, a right and a left. The rectangular pattern with a 45 degree entry leg will be studied in this manual because it is by far the most frequently used. Variations from this standard will be explained at the fields where they are used.

The pattern represents the glider's path of flight over the ground. Therefore, when there is a wind, corrections for drift are needed to make good the intended pattern. The pattern itself may also be brought closer or moved away from the field to suit wind conditions.

Throughout the pattern the pilot pays attention to his variometer. Lift is countered with cautious steepening of the angle of descent (see below), remembering that thermals close to the ground are apt to be small and to have sink around them. When sink is encountered, the pilot cannot count on moving again into compensating lift, so should bring the pattern closer to the runway and close the spoilers if they were opened before encountering the sink.

There is a well-founded rule that once a pilot has entered the traffic pattern he is committed to a landing and is not to be seduced away from it by the most enticing thermal. There are several reasons for this, one of which is interference with other traffic, another is the possibility of being blown away from the field while circling and then being unable to penetrate back against the wind, and a third is the undesirability of slowing to thermaling speed so near the ground.

Before taking up the traffic pattern and landings, a student learns to maintain a constant airspeed while changing the glider's angle of descent. This is a simple matter of blending a change in pitch attitude with a change in spoiler setting.* Nosing down results in an increase in speed if spoilers are left unchanged; opening spoilers results in a *decrease* of speed if the pitch attitude is left unchanged. These two speed controls—elevator and spoiler—can easily be managed to counteract each other so that speed is unchanged while the angle of descent is varied between the limits set by the flat glide of the clean wing and the steep descent with spoilers fully open. In doing this, the stick and spoiler control are moved slowly, smoothly, and *together*. Since the technique will be practiced every time a pattern is flown, proficiency will not be long in developing.

If at any point in the pattern the pilot is unhappy with his position or altitude he should not dawdle, but do something about it *at once.* If high he can steepen his descent or angle away from the field, or both. If low, he *must* move closer to the field, keeping his spoilers closed. If *very* low, the pilot should not hesitate to abandon the pattern, fly straight toward the field, and land in whatever direction seems safest to him. The traffic pattern is not an end in itself, but the means to an end, a safe landing.

THE ENTRY LEG

During any flight, a glider pilot always keeps track of wind conditions aloft and on the ground and plans so that he is able to reach the entry point at the specified altitude. A gliding turn is used for traffic pattern entry to help the pilot spot other aircraft. The altitude at the entry point should be from 800 to 1000 feet AGL. The entry leg is at 45 degrees to the downwind leg.

---

*A similar technique is used in flap-equipped gliders, discussed more fully in Chapter 16.

On the entry leg the pilot adjusts for proper spacing between his own and other aircraft and then trims to pattern airspeed. Spacing is accomplished by speeding up or slowing down. To move ahead of another glider, the speed should be increased to about 20 mph above the best glide speed, and if the altitude being lost makes it seem necessary, the pilot can move his pattern closer to the runway. To fall behind another glider, the speed should be decreased to slightly above minimum sink speed. The pilot should exercise a little judgment with respect to the normal speeds of different types of gliders in traffic. For example, it is unwise to squeeze a 2-33 trainer into the pattern ahead of a 2-32 or HP-11.

When traffic spacing is satisfactory, the pilot establishes his pattern airspeed, setting the elevator trimmer if the glider is so equipped. A suitable pattern airspeed* for any glider is 50% above stalling speed plus half the estimated wind velocity. Pattern airspeed is an *absolute minimum*, with a plus tolerance of ten mph for beginners and 5 mph for more experienced students; there is *no* tolerance on the low side. This pattern airspeed *must* be maintained until the final approach is flared out for landing.

If every glider pilot could be persuaded to follow the pattern airspeed rule to the letter it would virtually eliminate the entire category of accidents most dangerous to the pilot—the stall-ins and the spin-ins. No other subject received the earnest attention that was given to this rule by the many advisors who assisted in the preparation of this manual. It is recognized that no pilot *wants* to fly "too slow and too low", but many pilots have come to grief because they had mistaken ideas of what constitutes a safe minimum. The pattern airspeed rule is designed to provide such a minimum. If the reader will apply it *invariably*, this entire training manual project will have been worthwhile.

When the wind tends to blow the glider away from the field the traffic pattern should be brought in closer, and vice versa. This should be considered before starting to turn into the downwind leg. The altitude here should be 600 to 700 feet AGL.

On the downwind leg, the pilot checks the windsock and activities on the ground, looks again for other traffic ahead of him, determines his precise landing spot, and checks the operation of the spoilers by opening and closing them. A secondary reason for checking spoilers is to develop a habit against the day when he may fly a glider with retractable wheel. Landing gear warning signals are normally operated by the spoiler or flap control; the habit of checking may someday prevent a wheel-up landing.

When flying the downwind leg many beginners will stare over the nose of the glider as if hypnotized. Concern with the glider's attitude and airspeed are all very well, but they require only a fraction of the pilot's attention. He should also look down at the landing area, keeping track of his progress in relation to the runway, judging the angle downward along the three legs of the pattern to the point of flare-out, and estimating the effect of the wind on his glide path. The purpose of doing so is to develop a consciousness of the appearance of a correct approach from any point in the pattern under any wind conditions. Reliance on the altimeter is of no avail in an off-field land-

*It is a lamentable fact that there are wide variations in the accuracy of glider instruments, and especially the airspeed indicator. The causes are various and at this point unimportant. What *is* important is that the pilot who flies an unfamiliar glider learns the extent of the error of his airspeed indicator. It only takes a few seconds after release from tow to do a stall straight ahead with the pitch attitude no higher than required to produce the stall. Upon noting the *indicated* stalling speed, the pilot will have a basis for determining his minimum pattern IAS and the other important gliding speeds.

ing where field elevation is unknown. Dependence on the altimeter in flying the pattern should be overcome as soon as possible.

On the downwind leg, the pilot's immediate concern is planning the exact line of the base leg and the point at which to begin the turn into it.

THE BASE LEG

The turn into the base leg should be accomplished at 400 to 500 feet AGL. Here, it is especially important to complete the turn with the glider crabbing into the wind. If it were blown far back from the field at this low altitude the glider might not be able to penetrate into the wind to reach the field.

On the base leg the pilot is planning his final approach, remembering that the ideal glide path is midway in steepness between a full-spoiler and a no-spoiler descent, taking into account the strength of the wind. His object is to fly a base leg which will take him to this ideal final approach path. He adjusts the base leg to accomplish this end.

As soon as the turn to base leg has been made, the pilot is in an excellent position to check for traffic on final approach ahead of him by looking to both right and left.

Occasionally, for whatever reason, a pilot may find himself much too high or low; this should be apparent to him when he completes the turn into the base leg, and he should correct it immediately. Let's consider what should and should not be done when too high. This situation should be handled by nosing down and opening spoilers, by side-slipping away from the field and by angling the base leg away from the field and extending it beyond the normal point for turning into final approach. While doing all this, the pilot must keep the runway in view so he can judge the progress of his corrections. What he should *not* do is to make a 360 degree turn away from the field. The glider might move into

heavy sink or be blown back from the field, ending the circle too low instead of too high. Another practice that should be avoided is making "S" turns to lose altitude either on base leg or final approach. A number of accidents have befallen pilots who were "essing" off altitude, caused by poor technique, too steep banking, the unpredictable behavior of the air close to the ground, or an unhappy combination of the three.

When a pilot is too low on base leg he can forget about hitting his landing spot and concentrate on getting into the field for a safe landing. The instinctive reaction, of raising the glider's nose to "stretch the glide," has the opposite effect of steepening and shortening it. The correct course is: (1) close spoilers, (2) make a nose-low turn toward the closest point of safe landing, and (3) dive moderately to the lowest safe altitude. The object of getting low is to fly below the wind velocity gradient in a reduced headwind, and to benefit from ground effect. The altitude lost in diving is not wasted; it is converted into speed which greatly increases the floating distance.

A word of caution: this tactic is only to get the glider over the fence from the base leg. It won't work from greater distances, from which an alternate landing site should be chosen.

FINAL APPROACH

The final turn should be entered at 200 to 300 feet AGL. Here, great care should be taken with coordination, bearing in mind that a skid is less safe than a slip. Airspeed in the turn should err on the high side if at all. (Some schools require a nose-low turn into the final.) The bank should never be allowed to steepen beyond 45 degrees, while 30 degrees is normal and preferred. This particular turn is unforgiving of pilot error because of the low altitude.

With the turn completed, the pilot now directs his attention to landing reasonably close to his planned spot. Only a few years ago all

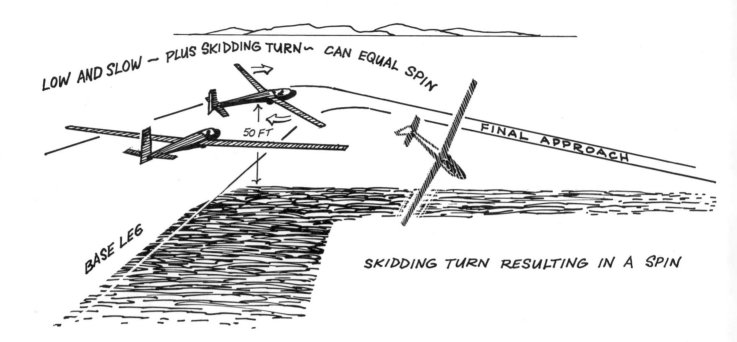

LOW AND SLOW ~ PLUS SKIDDING TURN ~ CAN EQUAL SPIN

50 FT

FINAL APPROACH

BASE LEG

SKIDDING TURN RESULTING IN A SPIN

schools taught that spot landing was accomplished by visualizing a line of flight from the final turn to the point of flare-out. The pilot then endeavored to fly down this imaginary path by manipulating his spoilers while controlling airspeed by raising or lowering the glider's nose with the elevators. The problem for a beginner was to detect soon enough any departure from the desired glide path (once he learned what it should look like), and to make speed corrections without creating other such departures. It wasn't easy. Even now, veteran pilots taught by this method still speak of continued spot landing practice to maintain proficiency.

Fortunately, an easier approach to spot landings has appeared, easier to teach, to execute, and needing little or no practice to stay in form. Most students learn this method in about one-third the time, and when ready for solo (after 30 flights as an average) are consistently landing within commercial flight test tolerances. This is how it is done.

The pilot selects a point on the runway about 50 yards short of the planned landing spot where he will flare out his descent. He now *aims* the glider at this flare-out point, keeping it aimed as the approach progresses. This aiming of the glider needs little or no instruction—it's as easy and natural as pointing your finger. (Some young people like to imagine they are "The Red Baron," aiming a machine gun at an enemy who is standing on the flare-out point. They never miss.) Meanwhile, the pilot uses the spoilers as necessary to control the airspeed, canceling out the effect of any change in pitch attitude caused by "aiming."*

---

*It may be protested that the elevator should be the only control used to govern airspeed. However, spoilers are legitimate speed-limiting devices within their range of effectiveness, and a pilot should not be prevented by tradition from using them as such. When speed increases despite full spoilers, a slip is indicated. When it decreases despite closed spoilers, the nose must be depressed.

When the glider is almost to the chosen flare-out point and at an altitude of 5 to 20 feet depending on the angle of descent, the pilot smoothly rounds out the glide so the flight path becomes parallel to the ground at an altitude of a foot or two. The steepness of the descent determines how much altitude is needed to flare out. From a spoilers-closed flat glide the change in pitch and angle of descent is minimal and requires little altitude. When coming in very steeply, with full flaps or spoilers and perhaps a little supplementary sideslip, the flaring out process must be commenced higher up. The absolute necessity of having full pattern airspeed is underlined at the flareout from a steep approach; if speed is less, the lift of the wing may be inadequate to check the descent and the landing may be hard enough to cause damage or injury.

When the flare-out is completed, the pilot transfers his attention to the planned landing spot. While floating toward it, he regulates deceleration with the spoilers, closing them to extend the float and opening them wider to shorten it. A helpful way to think of this controlling the length of the float is to pretend the spoiler handle is a throttle which extends the float when pushed forward and shortens it when pulled back. When within about 30 feet of the spot, the spoilers should be deliberately and smoothly opened all the way and the glider allowed to touch down in a level pitch attitude *without* using the elevators to put it down. The glider should settle down within a few feet of the spot. With practice and a little luck it may be within inches. (In a flight test the spot should be at the middle of the permitted landing area, while the spoilers should be opened fully as the line marking the area is crossed.)

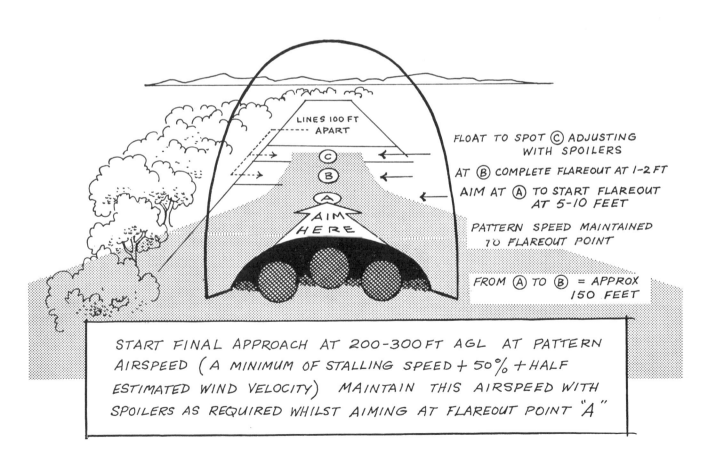

LINES 100 FT APART

FLOAT TO SPOT Ⓒ ADJUSTING WITH SPOILERS

AT Ⓑ COMPLETE FLAREOUT AT 1-2 FT

AIM AT Ⓐ TO START FLAREOUT AT 5-10 FEET

PATTERN SPEED MAINTAINED TO FLAREOUT POINT

FROM Ⓐ TO Ⓑ = APPROX 150 FEET

AIM HERE

START FINAL APPROACH AT 200-300 FT AGL AT PATTERN AIRSPEED (A MINIMUM OF STALLING SPEED + 50% + HALF ESTIMATED WIND VELOCITY) MAINTAIN THIS AIRSPEED WITH SPOILERS AS REQUIRED WHILST AIMING AT FLAREOUT POINT "A"

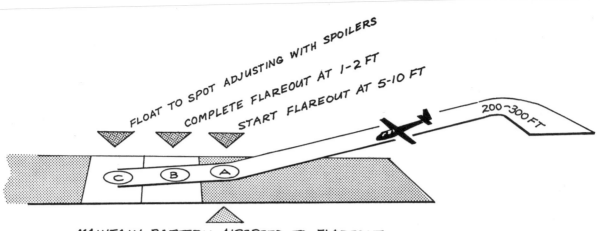

FLOAT TO SPOT ADJUSTING WITH SPOILERS

COMPLETE FLAREOUT AT 1-2 FT

START FLAREOUT AT 5-10 FT

200-300 FT

MAINTAIN PATTERN AIRSPEED TO FLAREOUT

In a glider equipped with adequate spoilers, that is the basic spot landing technique. Now let's consider some of the "*ifs, ands,* and *buts.*"

The most important consideration of the pilot on final approach is not to hit the spot, but to keep the speed at or above the selected pattern airspeed. This airspeed minimum *must* be maintained until the flare-out begins. The pilot should understand the effect of the wind velocity gradient (which may or may not be present) and of other atmospheric conditions near the ground, and *expect* the airspeed to decrease on final approach.* It is the normal situation. At the first sign of diminishing airspeed the pilot must close the spoilers as necessary, and be ready to lower the nose if that too is needed.

The objection might be raised that lowering the nose means that the glider will no longer be aimed at the flare-out point. This is true, but it will rarely cause the pilot to miss the selected landing spot. Having flared out seemingly too far back to float to the chosen landing spot, the glider now gets extra support from *ground effect.* The air between the wing and the ground is slightly compressed, providing the wing something more substantial than usual to work against. (Spoilers are still closed, of course.) The pilot stays as close to the ground as he can without touching down, and the glider just floats, and floats—and floats. Since the pattern airspeed has been carefully maintained right up to the flare-out, there is plenty of speed to be dissipated. When the glider is

within 30 feet of the landing spot the pilot will probably still have to open the spoilers to touch down.

When flying an early model glider with small spoilers, the pilot must supplement the drag of the spoilers with the drag of a yawed fuselage, and must aim the glider at the flare-out point even when the fuselage is cocked around in a forward slip.

The same procedure applies when crabbing into a cross-wind on final approach. In light to moderate cross-winds the wing-low side-slip is preferred over crabbing since it does not disturb the aiming concept. A strong cross-wind calls for both a wing held low and a crabbing wind correction. Just before touching down, the glider must be *ruddered* around to align the fuselage to the direction of motion. The upwind wing should be kept slightly low during the touchdown and rollout.

When a pilot thinks the cross-wind will be hard to handle, and he cannot land on another more favorable runway, he should align his final approach along the downwind edge of the landing area. As he flares out he should turn slightly toward the wind and land diagonally across the runway. Should the wind cause the glider to weathercock after landing, there would then be some room to avoid running into obstructions. When rolling, the rudder is used to control direction in the same manner as when rolling before take-off. The upwind wing is held slightly low also.

*Also see drawings and explanations on pages 59, 108, and 110.

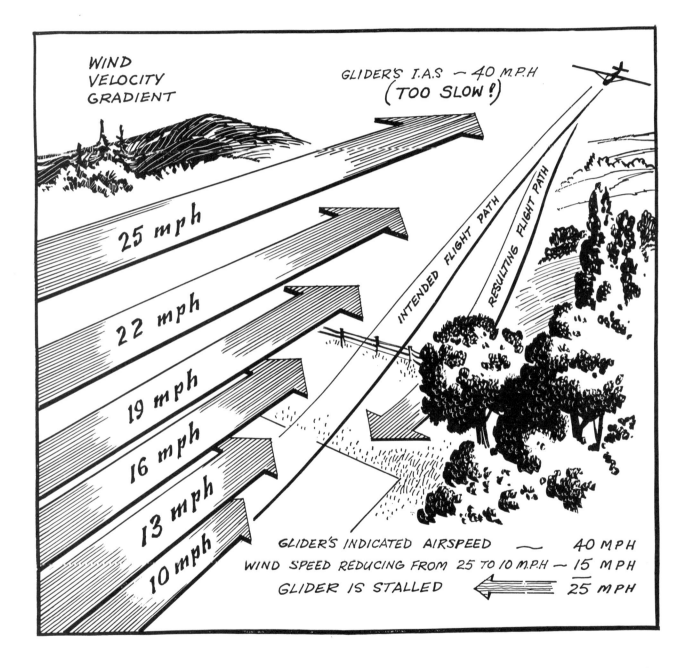

8. LANDING THE GLIDER

TOUCHDOWN AND ROLLOUT

The actual touchdown of the wheel is normally made while the glider is in a level pitch attitude, well above stalling speed. However, when floating in ground effect at an altitude measurable in inches, it is permissible to "hold it off" with the elevators to extend the float as far as possible, and to land with the tail slightly low. This technique is also used to make minimum speed landings on rough terrain, where the glider's lack of springs and shock absorbers might be felt below. The pilot should avoid flaring out too high and stalling the glider onto the ground; this is an abominable technique, quite liable to damage the bottoms of both glider and pilot.

Every day is "Be Kind to your Glider Day." On take-off and landing both, the pilot should strive to spare the nose skid as much rubbing as he can. This is unimportant on a lush grass field, but on paved runways or on unpaved sandy strips the wear on the nose skid can be prodigious. One school operator installed quarter-inch thick steel shoes on the skid, and they lasted a mere forty hours of instruction time. Understandably, this resulted in an immediate change in roll-out technique at that school.

Good judgment is shown by a pilot who can plan his landing spot correctly, land on it, control his rollout with spoilers only, roll slowly to his planned stopping place, and then come to rest with a gentle application of wheel brake. The brake must be applied smoothly to spare the tire as well as the brake itself.

Bad judgment is shown by turning off the runway at high speed, rolling rapidly into the tie-down area, and coming to a screeching halt on nose-skid and locked wheel. Either the brakes or the planning could be as weak as the un-common nonsense displayed by the pilot, with resulting damage to something.

DOWNWIND LANDING

With a light tailwind, under 5 mph, its effect on an approach and landing is very slight. The glider seems to be gliding a little flatter and faster in relation to the ground. The rollout also seems a bit quick, and control is lost a little earlier than usual. However nothing really exciting happens.

Things are quite different, however, when fate or bad judgment forces a downwind landing in a 15-25 mph tailwind. If this happens, the chosen landing spot should be near the beginning of the field, and in an uphill direction if possible, as the rollout will be long. The path of the rollout should be planned to be right down the middle of the widest part of the field, since the pilot will have serious problems of directional control in the last half of the rollout.

As the ground is neared, it sweeps by so fast that the pilot has an almost irresistible urge to raise the glider's nose and slow down. It takes real strength of character (and comprehension of the situation) to keep the airspeed up to pattern airspeed. The pilot has one thing working for him: the wind gradient, which is a hazard when landing into the wind, actually helps by increasing the airflow across the wing in a downwind landing. (If there *is* a gradient on this very special occasion.) The pilot must try to exclude from his mind the fast-moving scenery, and concentrate on keeping his indicated airspeed up. Flare-out and landing should be normal except for the unusually high groundspeed.

After touching down, the pilot should concentrate all his skill and attention on keeping the glider rolling perfectly straight until it comes to a full stop. Under no circumstances should he turn toward the side of the field, as is often done. Keep the wings level as long as possible. The wheel brake should be used firmly so long as the glider rolls straight. When the nose comes down (against the pilot's full back stick), the nose skid is helpful until the glider starts to swerve, when it may dig in and pivot the glider into a ground loop. Once a swerve is underway, locking the wheel will help, assuming the brake is in good enough condition to do so; anyway, use the brakes *hard*.

As the glider slows below the wind speed the airflow is across the controls from the rear. The function of the controls is abnormal, but the wind force can be used to oppose the tendency to swerve *provided* the pilot can remember the rule: if the swerve is to the right, push full right rudder and full left stick. Crossed controls. This is not the time for steering; we just want to oppose the swerving and try to roll straight. If it swerves *left* use left rudder and right stick. Elevators should now be depressed, i.e., stick forward, to keep the wind from lifting the tail.

There is no substitute for experience, and a student pilot near the end of his training, almost ready for his FAA flight test, should have enough *dual* downwind landings in safe winds (around 10 mph) to understand the situation, to fix in his mind the control use when the wind is overtaking the glider, and to acquire a basis for future decision-making in off-field landings.

SIMULATED OFF-FIELD LANDING

Simulated off-field landings are a must in training for the normal and expectable off-field landings of cross-country soaring. If possible, other landing areas should be found than those regularly used by the student. It must be assumed that the pilot does not know the exact field elevation, so the altimeter should be covered. The entire pattern should be planned and flown as usual, except that the placement of the legs and turnpoints must be planned by reference to the angle downward toward the landing spot, or how the field looks from the glider.

For the average off-field landing, the flare-out would be just inside the landing area and touchdown with full spoilers would follow soon thereafter. Therefore, the practice off-field landing should be done the same way. On final approach, aim for the fence, flareout so as to clear it, open spoilers fully, and land. When you get out of the glider, study the wind conditions and how much field you used, and file for future reference not too far back in the mind.

Above all, keep *full* pattern airspeed to the flare-out. The kinetic energy stored in that much speed can, with spoilers closed, float the glider a long way, perhaps clearing a ditch or rocks that were unseen from aloft, and allowing you to pick the exact place where the terrain is best for touching down.

CREWING

At this stage in the student pilot's training he should be looking for a chance to crew for an experienced pilot on a cross-country flight. Crewing can be both good preparation for the student's own future cross-countries and can also be lots of fun. This is especially so when two-way radio communication makes it possible for the crew to follow their pilot closely and share his tribulations, decisions and successes. Not the least of the sport is the after-landing dinner and the long drive home during which the flight is analysed and second-guessed far into the night. All glider pilots are natural-born members of the "If Ida Club." "If Ida stayed up in the mountains Ida made Diamond Distance for sure."

9. PRE-SOLO CONSIDERATIONS

ACTUAL OFF-FIELD LANDING

The student is now nearing the time for his first solo, after which he will be on his own in the event of a real off-field landing. This will seem quite different from the simulated variety, during which the instructor could be counted upon to pull the student's potatoes out of the fire. *Before* solo is the time to give the matter some earnest study.

When in the air, the student can select fields that he believes to be suitable for landing, and then later visit them by car for a closer look to see if the judgment was well-founded. Drives should be taken in spare hours for the express purpose of studying possible landing sites. In particular, he should look for obstructions that might interfere with an approach or damage the glider on the ground. Ground which has once been cultivated is much to be preferred over unimproved terrain. Watch out for: high tension line towers and telephone poles (the wires may be hard to see), trees, fences, irrigation pipes and sprinklers, highway markers, signs, and even mailboxes. Farm and ranch service roads may be excellent, though the road in from the highway is liable to have phone poles or fences beside it. If a suitable field can be found, a landing should not be made on the highway for several reasons including possible violation of state law. If a landing *must* be made on a road, the pilot should look for obstructions along the side, including graded embankments and those ubiquitous little stakes with reflectors on them. If seen in time, it may be possible to clear one and come to a stop before the next.

In regard to the tough decision of whether to land into the wind and downhill, or downwind and uphill, many instructors advise *never* to land downhill. They have the right idea, but "never" is a long time. The wind could be strong and the hill a gentle slope; moreover, the approaches might be the determining factor. However, when landing uphill the pilot can stop the glider fairly quickly, even from a high landing speed. Few experiences generate the feeling of utter helplessness felt by a pilot who has landed into the wind at moderate speed but rolls inexorably downhill, wheel brake fully set, toward some unyielding obstacle. In this situation the glider should be deliberately ground-looped by putting a wing down hard and applying full rudder. Damage will probably be less than from running head-on into an obstruction.

When in the air, a part of a pilot's mind should be on landing possibilities. At high altitude there need only be a general plan. When down to two or three thousand feet AGL the plans should be more specific. At pattern altitude the pilot should be committed to landing at the field selected when higher up, and he should proceed to land. There should be no flirtations with vagrant thermals below pattern entry altitude for some of the same good reasons which make this the rule at the home gliderport.

GETTING BACK TO THE FIELD

The glider pilot is concerned at all times with his angle of descent. Sometimes he is thinking in terms of numbers. For example, on a cross-country flight he might translate an altitude of 5000 feet AGL into the ability to glide 20 miles toward his goal. More often, though, in local flying as well as cross-country, the pilot is thinking in terms of an angle downward from the horizon, a visualized glide path that the glider can maintain under existing conditions. While weighing the effect of lift and sink, head and tail winds, and the capability of his machine, he is studying whether he can get back to the home field, or on cross-country, which fields he can reach with a safe margin of altitude. The ability to judge glide path capability develops with each flight, and with conscious observation and analysis. "No thinkee, no learnee."

Before a student soloes he should understand speeds-to-fly and have the data with him in the cockpit whenever he flies alone. See Chapter 13 and Appendix A. Speed-to-fly takes into account rising or subsiding air, but it does not consider head or tail winds since these have no effect on the proper speed between thermals. However, on a final glide, or a glide back to the home airport (which is a similar situation), wind does affect the most efficient glide speed. With a tailwind, the speed-to-fly is the *practical* optimum, though there may be a small theoretical advantage in flying slightly closer to minimum sink speed, depending on the glider's performance curve.

When bucking a headwind to get back to the field, the need to *penetrate* is urgent, and flying too slowly is a serious error. The approximate correct penetrating speed is the speed-to-fly plus half the estimated wind velocity at the glider's flight altitude. Since the penalty for gliding five (or even ten) mph too fast is negligible, the pilot should guess high in estimating the strength of the headwind.

The considerations discussed above are important at this juncture because, lacking experience, the newly-soloed student may wander away from the airport or forget his instructor's injunction to *stay upwind of the field*. Knowing the most efficient gliding speed under all con-

ditions will help him to get back. At the same time, bear in mind that a safe off-field landing is greatly to be preferred over a risky glide back to the airport.

PREFLIGHT INSPECTION

For all flights in which he is engaged, the instructor has the responsibility for preflight inspection of the glider. However, with his first solo, the student has the honor and responsibility of being Pilot-in-Command, and this includes the duty of making the preflight inspection.

A pilot has both the legal and self-preservational final responsibility of assuring himself of the airworthiness of any aircraft before he flies it. If he is unaware of the status of the glider, he should first examine the Registration and Airworthiness Certificates to see if it is legally flyable. Then he should read the Operations Placard to determine if Gross Weight and Center of Gravity will be within bounds as he plans to load the glider. (Lightweight pilots take special note.) This is a good time to look into the nose of the glider to see if ballast from a previous flight has been accidentally left there, or to add ballast if required. Don't shrug this off; your life may depend on it. When all is as it should be, the pilot can proceed with a check of the cockpit area. The procedures and checklists given below are for a conventional two-place training glider; other types would require changes in some details.

In general, inspect for condition, operation, security of attachment, signs of wear or looseness, and improper maintenance or assembly, all of the following:

Shoulder harness and seat belts

Canopy, its hinges and latches

Release mechanism. Check actual operation of both normal and emergency releases.

Function of all controls, verifying correct-

ness of response.

Instruments. Check pitot and static lines for insects, moisture and kinks in the hose.

The next step is to close the canopy and proceed with a walk-around check. The pilot should begin by stepping away from the glider a few paces to study it carefully for symmetry and for external signs of strain, i.e., bends in wings, struts, and empennage that could be missed at short range. Top and bottom wing skins as well as fuselage skin should be examined from close-up for wrinkles which would indicate that they have been stretched past their elastic limit. The rivets attaching wing skins to spars should be inspected for looseness or indication of strain. If the wing is painted, small cracks around the rivet heads give warning; however, wings which have been filled and painted may develop surface cracks in the paint from normal flexing which are no cause for alarm. The pilot should also, gently but firmly, shake the wings at the tips, all control surfaces, and also the stabilizer and fin. This can disclose improper attachment or excessive wear that could create a flutter condition in flight. Walk around the glider, inspecting:

Wings and attachment bolts

Center-section control connections

Struts and attachment bolts

Stabilizer, elevator, fin and rudder

Fuselage covering and structural tubing

Ailerons and spoilers

Main wheel, brake and tire

Tail wheel and bracket

All control cables and pushrods

Nose skid and metal shoe

Control locks removed and pitot head uncovered

Tow rope and condition of tow equipment may or may not be the pilot's responsibility, depending on circumstances.

Here are a few items that might have to be checked on more advanced gliders, not necessarily a complete list, either:

Radio operation

Oxygen supply and pressure gauge checked and turned on at the tank, mask in cockpit

Landing gear warning system functioning

Elevator trim control for proper response and setting

Variometer and audio device, function and adjustment

Condition of wingtip wheels or skids

It should be mentioned that utter perfection is as rare in gliders as in people, or nearly so. The pilot's duty is to call discrepancies to the attention of responsible maintenance personnel and then to decide for himself whether they affect safety in flight.

The inspection just described is mandatory before the first flight of the day. It is not a lengthy task, taking little more time than it does to tell about it. Between flights during the day, if a full preflight was done in the morning, a *short form* inspection will suffice. The pilot will walk toward and around the glider, studying it for anything unusual, in particular for evidence of a hard landing. All controls should be operated exactly as for a full-length preflight. Check the shoulder straps and seat belts while loosening them preparatory to getting in the glider. The before take-off checklist will complete the short form inspection.

A final thought regarding pre-flight inspections: younger pilots are sometimes a trifle scornful of the meticulous inspection habits of the grey-haired old-time pilots. The young should realize that this caution has contributed to their becoming old-timers—instead of statistics.

10. FIRST SOLO

When a student has completed the foregoing flight training and the accompanying ground school to his instructor's satisfaction, his student permit will be endorsed by the instructor to certify that the student is qualified to solo in the type glider for which he is deemed competent. At the same time, in a school or club which follows the SSA's ABC training program, he will have earned his "A" achievement pin. For details, see Appendix C. The A pin is a significant milestone along the highway to the joy of soaring.

Students approach their first solo flight with what might be described as mixed emotions. Excitement, pride, confidence and apprehension combine to make this a never-to-be-forgotten moment.

Instructors react quite differently to the occasion since they are accustomed to judging the competence of students, and have been through this event many times. They wouldn't dream of soloing a student who would cause them a moment of anxiety; it simply isn't necessary. The instructor knows from experience that the maneuvers which have been practiced and the good flying habits that have been developed will meet every demand of solo flight.

Having soloed, the fledgling pilot has proved to himself and to the world his ability to take a glider up and bring it back safely. Beyond this, "unfinished" would be a realistic description of his development as sailplane pilot. Before his license examination, there is still much to do. He should space periods of solo practice with frequent dual instruction so that his instructor can indicate the areas in his technique that need more polish and also give him instruction in soaring if conditions permit.

This is also the time to earn the instructor's endorsement for cross-country flight and if conditions warrant, to make a few short triangles and goal-and-return flights. Part II of this text deals with soaring and cross-country flying, but the student will have to rely on his instructor for advice on local soaring conditions and special information on other matters, including assembly, disassembly and trailering of the particular model glider being used for cross-country.

11. GLIDER TRANSITION FOR POWER PILOTS

The FAA requirement of ten flights for a total of two hours is enough for a competent power pilot to learn to handle a glider. If this flight training is supplemented by thoughtful reading of this and other books on soaring and by a realization that there is more to learn than mere control of the aircraft, then the transition may be accomplished safely.

Quite a few dented gliders bear witness to the fact that this is not always the way it works out. The trouble appears to be seated in the concept that checking out in a glider is just like checking out in another type of power plane, only easier. Admittedly, gliders are easy to fly, but this is the least part of the transition. The *big* job is to acquire soaring sense, which develops slowly from the experiences of many and varied flights. The way the wind affects the glide capability of a sailplane, what low-level turbulence and wind gradient mean to a slow-flying glider, the potentialities of thousand-foot-per-minute sink and many other conditions have to be experienced, digested and understood. To power pilots these conditions are relatively trifling, to be handled by a mere change in throttle setting. In gliders, these mat-

ters are the difference between pilot capability and incompetence.

In short, power pilots are often soloed in gliders and even licensed to carry passengers before they are aware of the facts of life in the sport of soaring. Worse still, they have no concept of what there is to learn.

When student pilots learn power flying they are taught the many ways of getting in trouble so they can develop good flying habits that will keep them out of trouble. When these well-trained power pilots come to soaring they should realize that this branch of the art of flying has its own peculiar problems, and good protective habits must be learned here also. *It is simply not enough to be a power pilot without power.*

* * *

The FAA flight tests for glider ratings are the same whether or not the applicant has power experience. Therefore the transition should include a review of the entire curriculum to be certain the pilot can perform each maneuver satisfactorily. Here are a few suggestions that may be helpful.

Coordination of stick and rudder in a glider

feels strange to the power pilot. The long wing accentuates adverse yaw, and the reluctance of designers to increase wetted area by providing large rudder area doesn't help the situation. For a given amount of aileron deflection, the amount of rudder required for perfect coordination is quite surprising. A good way to catch on to the relationship on the first flight is to do a few Dutch Rolls. (For the benefit of those without power experience, Dutch Rolls consist of simply rolling the wings 30 degrees each way without allowing the nose to move from its position on the horizon. The longitudinal axis of the glider must be kept perfectly stable while rolling around it.) After a few tries to get the feel of the rudder, Dutch Rolls should be abandoned in favor of the coordination exercises of the regular curriculum, which are more closely related to the needs of soaring. The advanced stage of this exercise, at maximum performance, will be sufficiently difficult to keep the most expert pilot on his toes. Because inaccuracy in coordination and poor control of airspeed affect glider performance immensely, the power pilot may have to set higher standards for himself than when his engine ensured forgiveness for his errors.

Many power pilots have never had spin instruction, in which case this omission should be corrected.

WIND GRADIENT

A STALL AND RECOVERY AT HIGH ALTITUDE RESULTS IN SMALL LOSS IN ALTITUDE

30 mph

25 mph

10 mph DIFFERENCE BETWEEN WING TIPS

20 mph

A STALL HERE RESULTS IN MUCH GREATER ALTITUDE LOSS BEFORE RECOVERY

15 mph

10 mph

TURBULENCE CAUSED BY GROUND OBSTRUCTIONS

THE RISK OF OVERBANKING NEAR THE GROUND IN A STRONG WIND

An important lesson in the transition to glider flight concerns the ability to fly safely at high altitude at speeds barely above a stall, and to thermal, making steep turns on the verge of an accelerated stall. At low altitude, such practices may cause a spin-in. The difference is not at all in the performance of the glider, but in the unfriendly behavior of the air close to the ground.

The prescribed traffic pattern and glide speed are shields against the adverse air currents near the surface. Any capable power pilot can easily fly any pattern desired by his instructor or the FAA examiner; but if he doesn't understand the special reasons why it should be flown that way in gliders, he may someday decide to do it differently and get in trouble.

The spot landing concept of aiming the glider may be new to some power pilots, though others say it is similar to their power approach. Some practice will be needed in aiming the glider at the flare-out point and controlling the airspeed by coordinating the elevator and spoiler controls. Being prepared for the effect of the wind gradient, ready to close spoilers and lower the nose if need be, will also be new to many power pilots who have been spoiled by that handy-dandy control, the throttle.

There are also many things to learn about navigation (primitive) and meteorology (local). Many power pilots are so used to the radio aids to navigation that they have forgotten all about the ancient art of pilotage. The crab angles normal to glider flight could startle a jet jockey. In meteorology, the U.S. synoptic weather map is of general interest to glider pilots but tells them very little about where to find the thermals that will support them. Here there is nothing to unlearn, but lots more to learn. To a beginner in soaring, the ability of our top pilots to find and utilize lift and to avoid or minimize the effect of subsiding air seems almost magical. These great sailplane pilots are experts in micrometeorology.

Summing up, ten 2000′ tows can be enough to win a glider rating for a power pilot under present FAA regulations, but it will take a lot more study and experience to transform him into a competent and safe sailplane pilot.

PART II   SOARING

Libelle H-301 — photo by Alex Aldott

12. THERMALING

ABOUT THERMALS

While our summer student is learning to handle the glider he will also be learning by observation and instruction the answers to these questions which wintertime students usually must get from text.

WHAT IS A THERMAL?

According to the dictionary, a thermal is "a rising air current caused by heating from the underlying surface." So thermals, in all their guises, have a common origin in heat.

WHY DOES HEATING MAKE THE AIR GO UP?

The air expands and becomes lighter, per unit of volume, than the surrounding atmosphere. It then rises like a hot air balloon, which is nothing but an enclosed thermal.

WHAT CAUSES ALL THIS HEATING OF THE AIR?

Primarily, solar radiation heats the ground, which in turn heats the air close to it by conduction. There are other less frequent sources of heat such as forest fires, steel mills and other hot factories, even a burning peat bog and a hot geyser.

DOESN'T THE SUN WARM THE EARTH ALL OVER?

Wherever its rays strike there is warming, but not equally. It depends on the angle at which the rays strike the surface, on the properties of the surface, on the extent of cloud cover, and even on whether the surface is wet or dry. Some knowledge of these considerations helps a glider pilot.

WHAT ABOUT THE ANGLE BETWEEN THE SUN'S RAYS AND THE SURFACE?

More heat reaches the earth when the sun is overhead than when near the horizon. What is less obvious is that the sun-facing slopes of hills get hotter than those where the rays slant across them. Thermals tend to rise over the warmer slopes and the air returns earthward where the sunshine is oblique or absent.

WHAT SURFACES ABSORB THE SUN'S HEAT MOST READILY?

It would take a good-sized book to deal with this question, a book that has not yet been written. Here are a few observations to supplement what the student may read elsewhere and learn from actual observation when soaring.

Color affects heat absorption; dark surfaces get hotter than light ones. Smooth surfaces get hotter than rough ones. Black-top highways, runways and parking lots are both smooth and dark, and may generate vigorous thermals. (For this reason, look for thermals over towns and cities.) Sandy beaches, dry river beds and smooth deserts get hotter than nearby rougher terrain. Vegetation does not get as hot as bare earth for two reasons: plants cool the air with the moisture they transpire, and their large surface area results in less heating per unit of area. Forests and green fields usually mean sink while nearby bare brown fields mean lift.

HOW DO WET SURFACES RESPOND TO SOLAR HEATING?

They don't get as hot as dry ones. Some of the solar heat goes to evaporating the water where the heat energy is stored in the water vapor perhaps to reappear later to fuel the growth of a cumulus cloud. Soaring pilots avoid rain whenever they can, and the wet areas that result from showers.

CAN A THERMAL BE SEEN?

Not with the unaided eye. However, a thermal may carry up objects which betray its presence and shape. Dust columns as high as two miles have been reported. Scraps of paper, flights of soaring birds, and even gaggles of sailplanes tell the same story. At the surface, dust devils, swirls of wind on growing crops or in the tree-tops of wooded areas, and smoke or dust converging from different directions mark the base of thermals. Last and most important is the cumulus cloud which (in its developing stage) marks the top of a thermal. When the cumulus is no longer fed by rising warm moist air it begins to evaporate, cool the air, and cause a down-draft. It is said to "decay", and in this stage can be pretty discouraging to the glider pilot who came to it counting on finding lift. The building cumulus has smooth swelling curves above and a flat or concave bottom. The decaying cumulus flattens above, losing its sharp outlines and becomes ragged below. One of a pilot's lessons of experience is to distinguish the stages of cumulus cloud development, and careful observation from the ground will help.

WHAT SHAPES ARE THERMALS?

They have no fixed cross-sectional shape. The shape of the hot surface which generates the thermal, and the effect of the wind determine the shape. Thermals can be bubbles which are warmed by the ground, swell, break free of the ground and rise like great hot-air balloons. Cool air then moves in from the sides replacing it, and there is a delay while this new air is warmed before the cycle repeats.

When the heating source is hot enough, it will be able to warm the air continuously, producing a column of a shape related to that of the heating surface—more or less. These thermal columns can be small and roughly cylindrical, or irregular in form and miles in extent. Bubble or column, the glider pilot tries to center his craft in the area of best lift. When he loses the thermal he can console himself with the thought that it was just a bubble.

HOW HIGH ARE THERMALS?

They go to the top of the highest thunderstorm, occasionally penetrating the base of the stratosphere to sixty or seventy thousand feet ASL. In the U.S., soaring pilots generally stay below cloud base, which could be substantially above 20,000 feet ASL in exceptional situations. From 3000 to 8000 feet AGL is a typical range of height for the cloud base in soarable weather.

DOES THE THERMAL CONTINUE INSIDE THE CUMULUS?

Yes indeed, and with greatly increased vigor. The latent heat of evaporation stored in the water vapor is released when it reaches the dew point and condenses. This source of heat energy provides the power that builds the giant thunderhead and the violent phenomena within it. This continues as long as the cloud is being fed by the rising warm moist air.

When the rising air is less moist and the resulting cumulus is small there may be little latent heat released. Under these conditions the lift may weaken before it reaches cloud base, sometimes to the degree that it will not support a climb to that height.

HOW FAST DOES A THERMAL RISE?

No one knows the precise maximum rate. Over 8000 fpm has been recorded in South America.

We can judge somewhat by the rate of climb of gliders. The weakest lift will merely slow the glider's descent. Very strong lift that "pins the needle" of the variometer, 1000 to 2000 fpm, is not uncommon in some parts of the country, and could be found in thunderstorms anywhere. The strongest lift must be far greater than the strongest actually recorded, judging from the fact that it could support a hailstone measured to be five inches in diameter.

WHERE DOES ALL THAT RISING AIR COME FROM?

When the thermal starts up, there develops a small low-pressure area at the surface below it. Cooler air rushes in from all sides to fill it. This can be demonstrated by putting pennants on poles around an area of black-top. When the pavement gets hot and starts producing a thermal, the pennants blow inward toward the center of the thermal.

WHAT BECOMES OF THE RISING AIR OF A THERMAL?

"What goes up must come down." When it reaches an altitude where it is no longer warmer and lighter than the surrounding air it stops rising and spreads out in all directions. It then settles back toward the ground, more slowly than it rose because the area of subsidence is greater. The fastest sink is close to the thermal, diminishing farther from it. When the lift is weak, so is the associated sink; strong thermals have proportionately increased sink between them.

DOES A THERMAL STAY IN ONE SPOT?

Only when there is no wind. At other times the thermal will move with the surrounding air, so a glider circling in it will be blown downwind. A horizontal wind shear may just tilt a thermal, or may break it up completely. A temperature inversion of sufficient magnitude will put a ceiling on thermal activity.

HOW DOES WIND AFFECT THERMAL FORMATION?

This depends on the balance between the wind velocity and the strength of the thermal. Weak thermals can be spoiled by light breezes and very strong thermals can stay together in a brisk wind. The range of winds that might be expected to end thermal soaring is about 15 to 30 mph. There are exceptional cases to make those average values look foolish, like most generalizations.

Downwind of obstructions such as windbreaks, small hills and even buildings, there is relatively still air in which thermals can be born and grow strong enough to penetrate through the higher wind above. These areas of "wind shadow", which must of course be sunny, should be sought out on windy days.

Soaring when a strong wind blows over very hot surfaces can be exasperating and baffling. The variometer shows frequent good lift, but the wind breaks up the thermals before the pilot can gain much altitude.

WHAT TIME OF DAY DO THERMALS COMMENCE?

Normally, between mid-morning and mid-afternoon. To answer this question a Weather Bureau Forecaster consults his chart of upper air soundings of temperature and humidity versus altitude and the temperature forecast for the surface. From these data he is able to predict with reasonable accuracy the triggering time and temperature, whether thermals will be strong or weak and the extent of cloud cover as well as the approximate height of the cumulus bases and tops. The strength of lift is related to the height to which it penetrates.

WHEN DO THERMALS SUBSIDE?

They cease only when the surface temperature cools enough to stop the process of launching heated air. The time is hard to forecast since the Weather Bureau can't know the temperature of every thermal-generating surface, or the different rates at which they cool down. In weak thermaling weather the lift may stop a couple of hours or more before sunset. On a strong day there may be isolated thermals after it is black dark. Cold frontal thunderstorms may provide ferocious but not very useful lift at any time of the day or night. Cloud cover can reduce solar heating and stop thermals at any time; so can an influx of stable air. There is no clear-cut answer to this question.

IS THIS ALL A PILOT NEEDS TO KNOW ABOUT THERMALS?

It is enough for a start. However, there is much more to be learned both from reading and soaring which will improve the pilot's ability and increase his pleasure.

*   *   *

THE BASIC IDEA

The glider's angle of bank and pitch attitude should be fairly well under the pilot's control, and the glider should be equipped with a variometer, airspeed indicator and altimeter. Thus prepared, the pilot can try his hand at thermaling. When the variometer reads up, the pilot commences circling, keeping a sharp eye on the instruments, the attitude of the glider and the position of other traffic. After a full turn he will know at what point of his circle the lift was best and where it was weakest. Mentally, he draws a line through these points, and then moves his circle toward the stronger lift to improve his rate of climb. When the variometer shows a constant rate of climb for a full circle, the glider is perfectly centered in the lift, so the rate of climb is best. Oh happy day! (It seldom happens.)

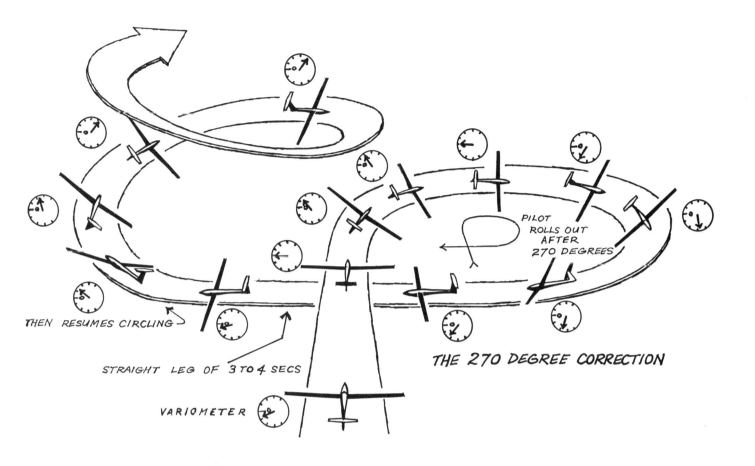

THEN RESUMES CIRCLING

STRAIGHT LEG OF 3 TO 4 SECS

VARIOMETER

PILOT ROLLS OUT AFTER 270 DEGREES

THE 270 DEGREE CORRECTION

THERMALING FOR BEGINNERS

Let's go back to the point where the variometer first shows a plus. At that point, the glider should be rolled *rapidly* into a bank which is no steeper than the pilot can control with ease—about 30 degrees is steep enough. The direction of the turn is not too important, but if a wing rises slightly as lift is encountered the turn should be toward the rising wing. The thermal is probably on that side.

Should the pilot turn in the wrong direction, the vario will soon show that he is going from the area of lift back into sink. To get back into the lift, the procedure is: (1) continue the turn in that same direction for three-quarters of a full circle, (2) level the wings and fly straight ahead for about 3 or 4 seconds, and (3) resume the turn in the same direction as before. This maneuver is known as *the 270 degree correction.*

The best airspeed for thermaling is the speed for minimum sink, which is usually about 5 to 7 mph above the stalling speed at the angle of bank being used. Any sign of pre-stall buffeting is a signal to increase speed slightly, not for fear of stalling but because the airflow over the wing is becoming turbulent, and greatly increasing the drag and the sink rate. Pitch attitude must be strictly maintained to avoid deceptive responses by the variometer to the pilot's small dips and climbs. These are called "stick thermals," and gain no altitude.

When noting the points of best and worst lift on the thermaling circle, consideration should be given to the lag of the particular variometer being used. This lag is easily determined by checking the delay in vario response after the pilot makes a sharp change in pitch attitude. A sluggish vario can be 20 to

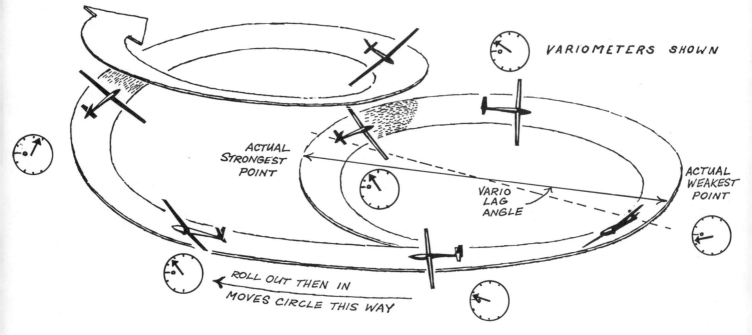

VARIOMETERS SHOWN

ACTUAL
STRONGEST
POINT

VARIO
LAG
ANGLE

ACTUAL
WEAKEST
POINT

ROLL OUT THEN IN
MOVES CIRCLE THIS WAY

CENTERING IN A THERMAL

30 degrees behind the progress of a steep turn, producing an equal error in the direction the pilot moves his circle if the lag factor is ignored. This would prevent the pilot from *ever* centering perfectly.

Having completed a full turn and located the strong and weak points, the pilot must now shift his circle to center it better in the thermal. The following is a good first method since it is uniform, effective, and unlikely to result in over-correction. Simply continue circling until the glider is heading in the direction the circle is to be moved, level the wings, and then immediately roll back into the turn. This maneuver will produce a small straightened section in the circle, thus moving the center. The next time around, the strong and weak points again should be noted and further correction made as needed. As previously hinted, one rarely achieves a *perfectly* even rate of climb around the circle, so thermaling is a continuing series of small corrections.

In all thermaling, the angle of bank should be changed *briskly*, using plenty of aileron smoothly applied. The coordination of stick and rudder should be the best of which the pilot is capable. The yaw string or ball should receive much attention.

Recall from the discussion of thermals that they are not necessarily simple round columns or bubbles. They come in many sizes and shapes and many even have more than one core. It is embarrassing to a pilot—when centered in one core of a thermal—to have another glider climb past in a stronger core a hundred or two yards away. The habit of exploring a thermal is a good one; this can be done by making frequent 360 degree turns at a reduced bank, say 10 to 20 degrees. These circles will carry the pilot away from his circling area and back again, so the thermal is not lost if the excursion proves unproductive.

MORE ADVANCED THERMALING

The foregoing concepts should be practiced by a beginner until—well, until he is no longer a beginner. In this period he should develop complete confidence in his use of the beginner's centering method (experts use it too) and of the 270 degree correction. His coordination will undoubtedly be much improved and he will be able to circle at his favorite rate of turn with his bank angle and pitch attitude closely controlled. His exploration of many thermals will have given him a fair idea of what to expect in different conditions. He should also have passed his second milestone along the highway to the joy of soaring by earning his B pin (see Appendix C). His greater competence means more fun and at the same time provides a base for further progress.

Now is the time to start varying methods to suit conditions. The purpose behind each of the following ideas is to achieve the greatest climb in the "leastest" time. This is an important factor in advanced soaring, since the optimum interthermal glide speed and the resulting cross-country average speed are linked to the achieved rate of climb.

The same centering method as was used when still a beginner may be modified now as the pilot learns to recognize the characteristics of the thermal he is working. He may roll level and fly straight for several seconds, watching the variometer closely, or he may wish to make a minimal correction and merely shallow the bank briefly. At first, corrections of this sort require much thought and conscious decision. After years of soaring a veteran instructor makes them almost subconsciously, and the beginner riding with him regards this as intuitive thermaling. It is not intuitive, but it requires only a fraction of the expert's attention, freeing him to consider other important matters.

Other ways of centering a thermal save time for the expert. Suppose a circle (perhaps even the first one) carries the glider right into the core of the thermal, and you feel that wonderful "whomp" in the seat of the pants, and the glider creaks acknowledgment. *Don't leave that very strong area!* Immediately "wrap it up tight" (which means to steepen the bank to 60 to 80 degrees) and make a half circle, but *no more.* Then shallow the bank to a more normal 40 to 45 degrees, assuming that the core is fairly small. The very tight half circle will shift the center of the thermaling turn into or near the center of the core. The time spent in weaker lift is reduced and the core is less likely to be "mislaid."

A different procedure may be followed when the pilot circles out into weaker lift or even into sink. He has a rough idea already where the better lift is, since he is in the act of leaving it. Turning back by reversing the direction of the turn is too slow. Once again, "wrap it up tight" and then roll out on a heading that will take you back into lift. Now watch the vario closely for signs of when to resume circling, and be alert for a wing-rise which would tell which direction to turn, since the location of the core may still be uncertain. Be careful at this time to apply no aileron which might hold down a rising wing "with a message."

These tactics will minimize the time spent in poorer lift and save seconds. Seconds are not to be scorned, like inflation-sized pennies. Seconds add into minutes and minutes into *miles.*

The beginner chose his thermaling angle of bank on the basis that he felt perfectly comfortable about his ability to hold it constant, producing round circles. Let's assume that our intermediate pilot feels at home in any angle of bank from 5 to 50 degrees. Now he can suit his bank to the thermal conditions as he deduces them from the indication of his variometer. Sometimes the lift area is very large and has no perceptible core; it is usually weak also. A bank of 15 to 20 degrees may give the greatest rate of climb as the glider floats lazily around at minimum sink speed. At the other extreme is the red-hot core of a small thermal, where best climb is attained by banking steeply, accepting the penalty of a higher sink rate to stay in the core. Choosing the bank is a pragmatic decision. The best angle of bank is the one that gives the best rate of climb in that particular thermal.

A beginner is well-advised to roll into a thermaling turn when he first has a plus on the vario. The expert will only do this when he feels that thermals are likely to be small. At other times he may fly straight while the lift increases, only starting to circle when it begins to diminish. Techniques in this respect vary both between pilots and with varying conditions.

Some pilots slow down as lift is first encountered, believing they can more easily evaluate the lift (a constant energy device is assumed to be a part of the variometer system) and more accurately roll in near the core. Other experts feel that slowing is a time-waster, preferring to keep speed high until a decision is made to work the thermal—or at least to give it a trial whirl. The reader can try both routes and come to his own decision. There *is* a potential time saving in the right choice.

Expert cross-country pilots fly much faster between thermals than do novices, except in very weak conditions or when they are desperately low. As a consequence they have devised techniques of pulling up and turning into thermals, both to convert the kinetic energy of the glide into altitude and to prevent losing the thermal because of the distance covered while rolling into a level turn.* The actual pattern of such a thermal entry depends upon the cruising speed, and also upon the pilot's esti-

*For a detailed analysis of these techniques see "Therm-ins and Therm-outs" in SOARING, issue of June, 1969.

mate of the probable size of the thermal and whether it is to the right, the left, or "don't know," as the pollsters say. Correct judgments and the best planned and executed thermal entries save many seconds *each time*.

When the pilot has no idea on which side the thermal is located, that is, he has not noticed the lifting of a wing, he can plan his pull-up and roll-in so as to locate his thermaling circle concentric around the point where he commenced the turn. Thus, a part of his first circle is deep within the thermal (which gives him a chance to evaluate its strength) and a part is well out in weaker lift or even sink. The alignment of weak and strong points tells him where the best area is. Or possibly he will elect to "wrap it up tight" as he goes through what he guesses is the best part without even completing the first exploratory circle. By such short-cuts more seconds are saved.

Time can also be saved when leaving a thermal. The beginner simply rolls out of his thermaling circle as nearly on course as he can and plods at near thermaling speed through the strongest sink immediately surrounding the rising air. This technique is costly in altitude, which of course takes time to regain. The expert will (when he is heading away from his course line) peel off in a tight 180 degree diving turn which takes him through the center of the core of the thermal just as he reaches his cross-country heading. Thus he accelerates while in the very strongest part of the thermal and then bashes through the surrounding sink at or above his cruising speed, pulling up and slowing to cruising as he moves out of the area of worst sink.

Note that these thermal entries and exits are aerobatic by *any* definition, so call for parachutes, adequate altitude, extreme caution with regard to other traffic and caution in avoiding heavy stresses on the glider, matters discussed more fully elsewhere in this manual.

The novice pilot usually stays in a thermal

until he has wrung every grudging foot of altitude out of it. The result is to reduce his average rate of climb, since thermals very often are weaker near the top. (Not, however, when the "top" is the base of a lively building cumulus.) Here is another of the expert's areas of decision. Unless there is some reason for doing otherwise, a veteran pilot will leave a thermal as soon as he is fairly certain the lift is weakening. A corollary to this idea is to decide the altitude band in which lift is strongest, as can often be done, and then to conduct the flight within that band so far as possible.

All thermals in a given area and time are *not* necessarily of the same strength, as is sometimes said. When an experienced pilot is at a secure altitude in good conditions, he may circle only in the best thermals, slowing but flying straight through the weaker ones. This delightful state of affairs can produce very high cross-country average speed. "Secure altitude" is wholly subjective, and what lift to work and what to reject depends both on conditions and the pilot's temperament, so no attempt will be made here to teach what may only be learned from experience.

13. CROSS-COUNTRY

PLANNING A PROGRAM

Once upon a time a pilot observed: "If I could win all the FAI Badges in one tremendous flight, I'd turn down the chance. Think of all the fun I'd miss!" A step-by-step progressive approach to learning cross-country flying is indeed more fun, and it is also the intelligent way to go about it. Each flight introduces some new problems, the solution of which prepares the pilot to attempt more ambitious goals.

Such a program might begin by flying preplanned triangles or squares around the home airport, learning to make progress from thermal to thermal and to fly at correct interthermal speeds. These short local flights also teach the effect of wind upon the glide angle. No problems of navigation or off-field landing are involved, since the pilot stays within gliding range of the airport and keeps his pattern mostly on the upwind side of it.

Before proceeding further with cross-country, the student will complete his ground school, including material found later in this chapter, and must receive his instructor's endorsement of competence to commence cross-country flying. He will also have earned the C pin, the highest recognition of progress in the SSA Training Program. The student can now cut the invisible cord that has tied him to his home airport and set out to earn the FAI Badges for distinguished soaring achievements which are described in Appendix D. He is now truly entering the world of joyous soaring.

A second step in a cross-country program could be a short goal-and-return flight to an airport ten or fifteen miles away on a day with little wind. This would allow an introduction to map-reading and flying a heading, but without risk of becoming lost. Pre-selected and inspected landing spots should dot the route like stepping stones so there would be no concern about having to land.

After this flight, a Silver Distance attempt should be made, or several of them if not immediately successful. The distance is only 50 kilometers or 31.1 statute miles. The FAI soaring awards rules should be consulted regarding the extra distance required when the altitude lost between point of release and landing exceeds 1000 meters or 3281 feet. This flight should be made downwind, not starting until the lift is reassuringly strong. The policy should be to get as high as possible, work all lift to stay there, glide at the speed-to-fly between thermals, and keep a good landing field within gliding range at all times. While an airport destination will allow an aero tow retrieve (very easy), an auto retrieve is better preparation for future flights since the glider must be taken apart and reassembled.

With Silver Distance attained, planning should be done for Gold Distance flights (300 km., or 186.4 statute miles) in several directions so the attempt can be made with a favoring wind whenever thermaling conditions are reasonably good. One day, perhaps even a most unpromising day, the conditions will be better than expected and the 187 miles will slip under the glider like magic. The pilot who waits for a booming day may *never* make it, and furthermore will not get the varied experience of the man who tries—and fails—often. The way to learn cross-country is to *go*, and go just as often as possible. Beyond a point, local soaring teaches little even though it gives much pleasure.

When the Gold Distance flight has been completed, the pilot is urged to enter local and regional competition if at all possible. This is urged as a part of the pilot's campaign to improve his skills, and regardless of whether he has the least interest in competition for its own sake or for the sake of winning. To learn, a pilot needs a yardstick by which he can measure his ability and find out his strengths and weaknesses. The performance of the other pilots, flying under identical conditions, provides such a yardstick, the only standard of comparison available in the world of soaring.

The most interesting, exciting and challenging stage of cross-country is the Diamond Distance flight, or "How far can I go?". This is a race against the sun, as a few minutes of arithmetic will amply demonstrate. As such, the early start, the favorable wind, the strong conditions, and all the concepts of time saving and flying faster are of deep concern. One cannot just stay up and float around all afternoon and log over 500 kilometers (310.7 statute miles). The joy of soaring reaches a peak in meeting this challenge, in learning how, in pouring unlimited enthusiasm and effort into successive attempts, until the day finally comes when all elements work in concert to produce a flight great enough to re-live on a winter's night, to tell your grandchildren about, and to earn the coveted Distance Diamond to add to your Gold Badge.

BEST GLIDE SPEED AND SPEED-TO-FLY

Earlier, the phrase "correct interthermal speeds" was used in connection with practice flying near the home airport. "Correct" is not an absolute, but a highly variable concept. What is correct for a Silver Distance flight would be quite incorrect for a Diamond Distance attempt or a competitive speed triangle. New terms and concepts are involved which are unfortunately somewhat confusing. The reader is urged to make the effort to grasp the distinctions as they are essential to an understanding of cross-country flying.

Best Glide Speed is a term that was long ago preempted by the aviation industry to signify the indicated airspeed which results in the flattest glide angle for a particular glider *in still air*. It is a point on the glider's performance curve. Best glide speed is rarely "best" for the cross-country pilot since he seldom flies in truly still air, and besides, can fly somewhat faster with a negligible penalty in altitude lost per mile. When the atmosphere has vertical motion, which is usually the case when thermaling conditions prevail, best glide speed never yields the flattest glide. At any given rate of vertical motion of the air, whether up or down, there is only one corresponding airspeed, called the *speed-to-fly*, that will result in the flattest glide angle. In sink, this speed is higher than would be best in still air. In rising air, the speed-to-fly will be slower, but not less than the speed for minimum sink. A method of calculating speeds-to-fly from any glider's performance curve is given in Appendix A. The accuracy of the solution depends on the accuracy of the performance curve. 'Nuff said.

Head and tail winds have no effect on speed-to-fly in cross-country interthermal flight because what might be gained between thermals is lost in the next climb, and vice versa. If there is to be no further thermaling, as in a final glide, then head and tail winds do affect the speed for flattest glide. Headwinds require a faster glide, and tailwinds a slower one. The correct term for this speed is simply speed-to-fly in wind. The exact value is a matter of arithmetic (or graphic solution) provided one knows accurately what the wind is. As a prac-

tical matter, the glider pilot usually has only a rough notion of the wind at his altitude, so precise calculations are rather futile. A reasonably good approximation is sufficient. Here is a rule of thumb: for headwinds, speed up by half the estimated headwind, keeping the estimate on the high side; for tailwinds, slow down by half the estimated tailwind, keeping the estimate on the low side, but never fly slower than the speed for minimum sink.*

Notice that best glide speed and speed-to-fly are terms with special and limited meanings. Just as best glide speed does not always yield the flattest glide, so speed-to-fly is not always the experienced pilot's choice, because the flatness of the glide is not his *only* consideration. In severe sink, the speed-to-fly might be overly fast for existing conditions of turbulence, creating a danger of over-stressing the glider. On the other hand, in strong thermal conditions, a pilot trying to make a high cross-country speed might decide to sacrifice some flatness of glide in favor of more speed, knowing he can quickly regain the lost altitude in the next thermal. This subject is in the realm of policy, and will be discussed further in "Flying Faster", pages 80-82.

For the early cross-country flights discussed here, up to and including Gold Distance, all interthermal gliding will be done at the speed-to-fly, with the margin for pilot error held on the high side (plus 5 to 10 mph is close enough). Under no circumstances glide *below* the speed-to-fly except on the final glide after the last thermal of the day, or in turbulence. This policy will provide the greatest chance of finding other thermals, the most likelihood of

---

*The reader may notice the inconsistency with the advice given the newly-soloed student. The benefit of flying slower in a tailwind is trifling, and it was not thought wise to ask a pilot at this level of experience to remember so much.

staying up, and the flattest glide after the last thermal. The average speed won't be too bad unless the thermals are excessively weak, in which case the pilot "should have stood in bed."

NAVIGATION

The student pilot properly learns about map preparation and the terms and practices of dead-reckoning navigation in his ground school. Often this instruction is keyed to powered flight, in which a constant altitude can be maintained, winds aloft are relatively unchanging, and the assumption can be made that if you went "X" miles in the last hour you will do the same in the next hour. Nothing could be farther from the facts of soaring flight.

Another assumption is that the compass has been swung (compensated) and a table of residual deviation placed on the instrument panel. This is seldom seen in gliders, though compass compensation is certainly a desirable practice.

Notwithstanding the above, much that the pilot has learned in ground school is applicable to soaring. Map preparation is one of these things. A course line should be drawn and marked at five mile intervals. The true course should be measured with a protractor at the meridian of longitude nearest the center of each leg of the flight (assuming there is a turn-point). Magnetic course should be calculated and marked near the course line. (Add Westerly, subtract Easterly variation.) If a compass correction card is in the cockpit, the compass heading is usually figured in the air, though it could be marked on the map ahead of time. The practical use of this part of flight preparation is limited to conditions of poor visibility (rather unusual in soaring), when the compass may be used to head the glider in the right direction long enough to pick out the farthest clearly visible landmark on course. After flying to this point, the pilot can repeat the procedure.

The more casual (and usual) use of the compass is for a quick check, upon leaving a thermal, that the pilot has not become disoriented while circling and made a gross error of direction. Such errors are easy to make in some parts of the country which lack prominent landmarks, especially when the sun is nearly overhead. At the start of each leg of a flight the pilot merely picks out the farthest identifiable check point along the course line, holds the glider steady until the compass settles down, and then reads the mid-point of its remaining oscillations. This heading will then be used for the rest of that leg as a check after thermaling or to help pick out other check points ahead.

Returning to map preparation, the most important factor is to study all the features marked on the map, and to learn to relate them to what is seen from the air. Glider navigation is not dead-reckoning but "pilotage," the principal factor of which is skill in map-reading. Until this skill is well-learned, careful study in advance of a flight is required. (It's not a bad idea at *any* stage of the pilot's development.) The first step in learning is to become thoroughly familiar with the chart itself, front and back, memorizing the various symbols used. The next step, for a beginner, is to drive along the course of a planned flight and relate as many as possible of the map indications to the ground features they represent. Except in the flatlands, special attention should be given to contour lines on the map which describe the topography almost as well as a 3-dimensional relief map.

One other practice of dead-reckoning navigation has great value to the glider pilot on a cross-country. This is to mark a trail of fixes on the map, with the time of passing, as often as accurate positions can be determined. The benefit of this is that if visibility worsens, or fatigue and circling confuse the pilot, that trail of fixes on the map will help greatly in keeping track of his position.

The analytical glider pilot, who may keep a barogram of each flight for later study, should mark each fix with the time and altitude. (Two zeros may be omitted from the latter.) For example, X $\frac{1505}{38}$ means that "X" marked the glider's position at 3:05 PM at 3800 feet ASL. The pilot may also wish to indicate by some symbol the location of each major climb in a thermal. With map and barogram, the flight may be reconstructed, mistakes analyzed, and much can be learned that will improve future in-flight decision making.

WEATHER

Federal Aviation Regulations, Section 91.5, require a pilot to be familiar with available weather reports and forecasts before any flight not in the vicinity of an airport. Neither of the key words, "available" or "vicinity" are defined, so a telephone call to the nearest Aviation Weather Forecaster or Flight Service Station, or even listening to an aviation radio weather broadcast would probably satisfy the law.

What will satisfy the glider pilot is another matter, and one which varies widely between pilots and with the character of the planned flight. For a conservatively planned cross-country in which the glider will always be within gliding range of an airport, all the pilot really *needs* to know is the wind direction aloft and whether conditions will be soarable. From this minimum, the weather information a pilot would like to have will increase with the ambitiousness of the proposed flight.

When a long flight is planned, the pilot will want an idea of the synoptic situation, of fronts, airmass types etc. He would like to know that the lapse rate along his route is not too stable, that cloud cover is not liable to become too extensive during the day, that the wind direction will remain favorable, and that no hazardous condition will develop. He will be interested in the height of cloud base or

the expected top of convection, and also in the time and surface temperature when useful thermals will appear. (Some forecasters assume this to be when the surface warms so there is a spread of 22 degrees Fahrenheit or more between the surface and 4000′ AGL.) A forecast of a high cumulus cloud base or tops of dry thermals means the lift will be strong, and so favors a long and fast flight.

With good reason, soaring pilots tend to become weather buffs, and some of our best pilots are very sharp indeed in meteorology. After all, nothing is more important to the success of a flight than the weather in which it takes place. While this manual is not primarily concerned with meteorology, it *is* concerned with helping the pilot to be successful in soaring. To this end, the pilot is urged to learn all he can about weather, particularly the local phenomena which determine the presence or absence of lift of whatever kind—waves, thermal, frontal, ridge, shear line, or whatever. He will want to keep up with articles in *SOARING* and to look up the very fine material to be found in back numbers. Also, as a very minimum, he will want to read the books on weather which are mentioned in Appendix E, Suggested Reading List.

So far, most Aviation Weather Bureaus have not had a great deal of experience with soaring forecasts and few of the forecasters are soaring pilots. This puts upon the soaring community a responsibility to report the soaring conditions actually encountered after a flight for which a forecast has been made. This will help the forecaster learn about soaring requirements; at the same time, the pilot will be learning what correlation exists between the forecast and the actual soaring conditions along his route.

"SOME PILOTS ARE RELUCTANT TO DEPART —"

CROSS-COUNTRY WITHOUT FEARS OR TEARS

Only a very few schools or clubs offer dual instruction in cross-country soaring, so it is only natural that some pilots are reluctant to depart *solo* from the security of their familiar home gliding area. The reasons for this reluctance are individual to each pilot, but surely the most frequent is a concern about being obliged to land away from an airport. This worry can be overcome (in most parts of the country) by planning the flight so as to stay within gliding range of an airport at all times. Minimum altitudes are calculated and marked on the sectional chart. The pilot who stays above these minimums can glide safely back to the last airport until he reaches a *go-ahead point* beyond which the next airport is in easy gliding range.

Longer flights, up to Gold Distance, are planned by breaking them down into a series of short legs, each prepared in the same way. Still longer flights could be made similarly, but by the time a pilot has earned his Gold Badge he will have seen so many landable fields from the air and will have gained so much confidence in his ability to stay up and make progress that he will probably have declared his independence of the requirement for an airport landing.

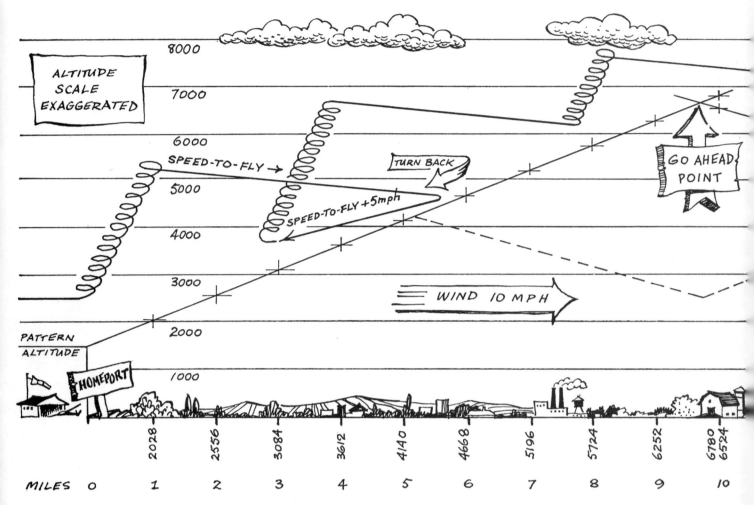

To illustrate this worry-free introduction to cross-country soaring, consider the planning of a hypothetical flight in a 1-26 in which the pilot leaves Homeport (elevation 500' ASL) and after 22 miles passes over Firstburg Airport en route to some more distant goal. In calculating the altitude minimums (a sort of flight profile), the pilot should assume a glide ratio of about half the maximum capability of his glider because if he should run into sink he might be unable to do better. For the 1-26, a ratio of 12 to 1 would be used for calm weather, 14 to 1 with a 10 mph tail wind, and 10 to 1 in the reverse direction. The flight plan should be based upon arrival over each airport at 1000' AGL to provide for a normal traffic pattern. Cheerfully assuming a 10 mph tailwind, here are the two glide tables that would be calculated:

Back to Homeport (Allow 528' per mile)		Forward to Firstburg (Allow 377' per mile)	
Miles from Homeport	Minimum Altitude ASL	Miles from Firstburg	Minimum Altitude ASL
1	2028	1	2377
2	2556	2	2754
3	3084	3	3131
4	3612	4	3508
5	4140	5	3885
6	4668	6	4262
7	5196	7	4639
8	5724	8	5016
9	6252	9	5393
10	6780	10	5770
		11	6147
		12	6524
		13	6901

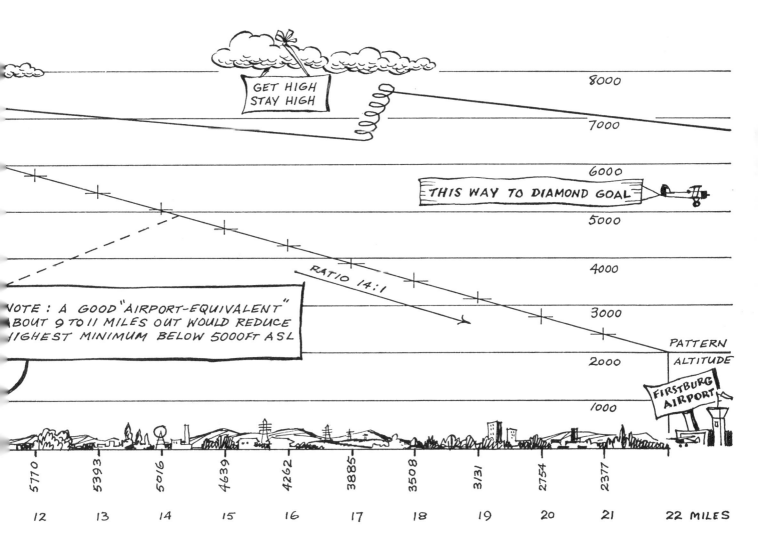

From a point 9¾ miles out from Homeport, at 6648 feet ASL the pilot could glide with equal ease back to Homeport or on to Firstburg. This is the go-ahead point. Altitude minimums should be marked at every mile up to the go-ahead point, but are not needed beyond, since Firstburg Airport can be reached easily even in subsiding air.

Occasionally two airports are so far apart that the go-ahead point is higher than one could reasonably expect to climb. In this case an airport-equivalent should be located between them. This is best done by car or plane, with a friend to drive or fly so the pilot is free to study the terrain. Consideration should be given to the approaches and surface, availability of a phone, accessibility to a retrieve car, and landmarks to help find the field from the air. The location of the field should be carefully marked on the pilot's and crew's maps.

Many farms and ranches have landing strips that are not marked on the charts. Freshly cut hay and grain fields and many pastures make excellent airport-equivalents, while in the West there are dry lakes. What is most important for this beginner's flight is that the pilot should feel as secure landing there as he would at any of the airports along the route. If he cannot find such a field, the route should be abandoned for the time being and another chosen.

Here is a policy statement for this worry-free cross-country:

1. Up to each go-ahead point, be mentally prepared to turn back if you get down to an altitude minimum. There is always another day.

2. After each go-ahead point, forget about the airport behind and concentrate on reaching the next one at a goodly height so as to have an advantageous start on the following leg.

3. When soaring with the wind, fly just over the speed-to-fly. If returning to an airport against the wind, increase the speed by half the estimated wind velocity.

4. Watch the vario when gliding back against the wind. You may find a thermal that will permit you to resume the flight.

5. "*Get* high and *stay* high," one of the prime axioms of soaring, has special relevance to the delightful downwind dash. This policy, if successful, frees the pilot from concern about an imminent landing and takes him up where tailwinds are likely to be stronger. The effect of lower atmospheric pressure is to increase true airspeed and cross-country speed. Rate of sink is increased, but so is forward speed, leaving the glide ratios at various *indicated* airspeeds unaffected.

FLYING FASTER

Long before he passes his FAA glider flight test, a student becomes aware that gliders are being flown between thermals at speeds far higher than the manufacturer's stated best glide speed. Altitude is like money—"easy come, easy go." Strong thermal conditions allow the pilot to spend his altitude riotously, knowing it can be regained quickly in the next thermal.

A pilot can earn his Gold Badge and two Diamonds (altitude and goal) without ever flying more than a trifle over the speed-to-fly. However, the time usually comes when he wants to enter a contest, go after the Distance Diamond, or have a friendly race with a soaring comrade. At this point he would like to know how to fly faster without driving his glider to the ground. Here are a few statements for him to mull over:

1. All the books on soaring explain the mathematical relationship between interthermal glide speed and the achieved rate of climb in the *next* thermal. The math is correct, but the assumption that the pilot knows what the next thermal will be like is just a happy dream.

2. It is well-known that the nation's top competitive pilots are anything but unanimous on the theory or practice of interthermal airspeed, except that they all go fast when conditions are good. Some simply fly a constant speed. Others use a MacCready speed ring, but where they set the index mark is a trade secret. One famous pilot who detests formulas has a formula of his own: to fly at whatever speed produces a rate of descent to match his rate of climb in the day's thermals. All these various ideas work for their protagonists who otherwise would not be at the top of the competitive heap.

3. It is pretty well agreed that as a pilot gets lower he should fly slower—and be less choosey about the strength of thermal he will work. At some certain altitude, individual to the pilot, he will be flying near the speed-to-fly and will gratefully accept *any* lift.

4. The keystone of fast flying is the ability to climb fast in thermals. The best pilot in the world can't make a high average speed when he can only climb 100 fpm. The ability to locate strong lift opens the door to higher cross-country speed.

5. The speed-to-fly produces the flattest glide; it does *not* produce either the fastest cross-country speed or the longest flight. The decision to fly faster is a

subjective judgment of the pilot, based upon his skill in analyzing conditions ahead as much as upon his present situation. Above all, his policy reflects his own temperament. This is not for one minute to imply that our fastest pilots fling away their altitude recklessly; they *must* stay up to finish and to win.

Absolutely none of the above is comforting to the beginner at flying faster. The implication is that he should go get some experience and stop being a beginner. Alas, there is some truth in this, but there is one simple tool to help him experiment, learn, and grow in experience. This is a knowledge of the cost in altitude of flying faster than the speed-to-fly. If the pilot knows the price tag on extra speed he has some basis for deciding how much to buy. Without that knowledge it is a shot in the dark.

The altitude lost *per mile* in the useful range of the glider's speeds (by 5 mph steps) can be derived from the performance curve. The speed-to-fly is apparent from the results (it checks with the easier graphic solution of Appendix A) as well as the additional altitude lost by flying faster. To get the complete picture, this calculation should be done assuming a reasonable range of convective conditions by steps of 100 feet per minute. These data are then plotted as a family of curves on a single sheet of graph paper.

To illustrate the computation of a single curve, let's assume a 1-26 loaded to 575 pounds gross weight which is gliding in sinking air of 100 fpm, a condition typical of a fine soaring day. The explanation of the figures will be found below the table.

A	35	40	45	50	55	60	65	70	75	80	85	90
B	159	162	174	192	216	246	282	327	378	435	498	570
C	259	262	274	292	316	346	382	427	478	535	598	670
D	1.73	1.5	1.33	1.2	1.09	1	.923	.857	.8	.75	.706	.666
E	448	393	365	351	344	346	353	366	382	401	422	446

Key to the computation:

A Indicated airspeed of the glider applicable to the figures below in each column.

B Glider rate of sink in feet per minute from Schweizer's performance curve, the graph in Appendix A.

C Same as B, with 100 fpm added for the subsiding condition of the air; this line would be changed when calculating the other curves of the series. These figures give the variometer reading at each speed.

D Minutes required to fly one mile. Line C and D are multiplied to arrive at line E.

E Feet of altitude lost per mile for each flying speed. These are the figures which should be plotted as a curve versus indicated airspeed.

Now we have the information we need for this one condition of subsiding air. Notice how different these figures are from the variometer readings. The speed-to-fly resulting in the flattest glide for this degree of sink is 57-58 mph. The cost of flying faster can be tabulated as follows:

5 mph — 5 feet per mile
10 " — 15 "   "   "
15 " — 29 "   "   "
20 " — 47 "   "   "
25 " — 67 "   "   "
30 " — 90 "   "   "

Some other interesting relationships appear from line E of the table. Notice that flying at minimum sink speed of 35 mph is 2 feet per mile more costly than barreling along at 90 mph. Notice also that flying 15 mph over the speed-to-fly costs only 29 feet per mile. In ten miles, a good unit for evaluating the cost of more speed, the extra altitude lost is only 290 feet, or about one minute's climb in a medium-strength thermal.

Organizing this information for any glider should take no more than one evening's work, especially if a slide rule is used systematically to perform the multiplications for line E. However, using the information, it could take a pilot a whole soaring season to decide upon a policy for cruising speeds which will represent his own personal compromise between boldness and conservatism. In deciding, he will at least have something better to rely on than the simple injunction to "fly faster".

LONGER FLIGHTS

Consider the arithmetic of a Diamond Distance flight, 500 kilometers or 310.7 miles. The time required is at least:

10 hours at 31.1 mph
9 "   " 34.6 "
8 "   " 38.9 "
7 "   " 44.4 "
6 "   " 51.8 "
5 "   " 62.2 "

These average speeds are made more difficult because the flight must be made partly in the weaker conditions early and late in the soaring day. A helpful factor is a good tail wind, but the benefit is limited by the fact that a too-strong wind will break up the thermals and terminate the flight.

The reader cannot expect this or any other book to teach him how to earn the third diamond, the *hard* one. This flight requires an all-out effort to achieve the highest average speed for the longest possible time. The best that can be done here is to offer a few reflections about this most fascinating subject—soaring for distance—which may help the reader plan and carry out a successful flight.

1. Make the effort to get in good physical condition before the soaring season. Long flights are very tiring, and a worn-out pilot makes poorer decisions than a fresh one.

2. Study the maps carefully before a long flight. Auto reconnaissance of the route is well worth the trouble if it can be arranged. This is something to do in the wintertime, when soaring opportunities are scarcer.

3. Pilot comfort is not just important, it is essential. Seating comfort, food, water and pilot relief should all be provided for.

4. Regarding the sailplane: our most numerous type, the 1-26, is capable of Diamond Distance in ideal conditions. There have been four or five such flights, one of which failed to earn the Diamond because of the altitude penalty. At the time of writing, several pilots are reported to be making a determined effort to earn the Distance Diamond in a 1-26. It is a terrific challenge; but if a pilot is more interested in the Diamond than he is in that particular challenge, he may be forgiven

for flying a sailplane of higher performance.

5. The sailplane should be carefully wiped off and taped to minimize parasitic drag.

6. Probably there is no part of the U.S. except Alaska and Hawaii where a Diamond Distance flight is impossible, and perhaps even Alaska should not be excepted. However, no one would deny that it is easier in some areas than in others. A vacation spent in Marfa, Pearblossom, Colorado Springs or some other outstanding soaring location just might make it easier to win the elusive third Diamond.

7. A long flight requires a long day. The pilot will have the best chance between the middle of May and the middle of August, although the long flight is possible at other times.

8. Good weather conditions are essential. Perhaps more Diamonds have been won (for distance, of course) in the unstable air a day or two after the passage of a cold front than under any other weather situation. A good tail wind is like money in the bank.

9. Carry oxygen in the glider and use it above 10,000 feet ASL. Good in-flight decisions come slowly if at all when a pilot is affected by hypoxia.

10. The use of a cross-country preparations checklist is desirable. Murphy's Law applied to soaring says: "If it can be forgotten, it *will* be forgotten—when it is most needed."

11. The early start is important. If sailplane pilots have any one fault, perish the thought, it is not being ready to go when worthwhile lift appears. With planning and luck an unusually early start may be possible. One such flight (373 miles in a 1-26) began early in wave lift and ended using thermals. Some early starters leave the airport as soon as they are fairly sure of staying up, merely drifting with the wind while waiting for the thermals to strengthen. There are other schemes, perhaps one the reader will dream up for himself.

12. Make the highest release from tow possible without incurring an altitude penalty, considering the altitude of the hoped-for landing area.

13. Plan ahead. At every stage of the flight the best course of action must be thought out. The pilot cannot just ride in the glider like a sight-seer, waiting for something to happen.

14. Explore under the first cumulus for the area of best lift. Subsequent cu's on the same day will likely have a similar structure and the pilot can go straight to the strong area without loss of time.

15. Don't waste time. Use all the time-saving techniques suggested in this manual, plus any you may glean elsewhere, plus those you can dream up yourself.

16. Below 2000′ AGL, work any lift, even the weakest, and when searching fly no more than 5 mph over the speed-to-fly.

17. Deviate from the course line (within reason) to follow the best lift areas. Follow cloud streets and try to stay out of the blue sky areas between the streets since they are often where the rising air of the cloud street returns to earth. When flying in steady worse-than-average sink suggestive of such a return flow (assuming there are no clouds to mark the existence of thermal streeting), turn 90 degrees away from the wind direction and you may run into a parallel area of lift—the unmarked thermal street. It's a gamble worth taking, since no good will come of continuing in the heavy sink.

18. When weather conditions look different ahead, slow down to conserve altitude. Speed up again if the suspect area turns out to have good lift.

19. Keep to the high ground. This old axiom of soaring is as reliable as ever. Lift is easier to locate and is usually stronger over the mountains than over the flatlands.

20. Avoid flying *through* a front; it will usually end the flight. Soaring can be fantastically good parallel to and ahead of a cold front. Warm fronts are usually no good from any angle.

21. Keep your eyes open for soaring birds; they find the best lift as though they could see it. Maybe they can.

22. Fly accurately, both as regards coordination and airspeed.

23. Avoid large wet areas, whether wetted by showers or irrigation. Large areas of green fields or woods are liable to be poor. If possible, pass along the upwind side of such areas.

24. Avoid areas shaded by high cloud or thunderstorms. If necessary, zig-zag to follow the upwind side of sunny areas.

25. Enter and leave thermals efficiently.

26. Alter the airspeed in interthermal gliding when the variometer reading changes. A well-adjusted constant energy device is a big help in cross-country flying.

27. Late in the day, stay high so as to have the longest possible final glide, as well as to avoid a premature landing. It is worth slowing up a little to stay high.

28. Naturally the pilot will want to fly as late in the afternoon as lift conditions permit. The Law, the safety of the glider, and the pilot's neck all demand a little prudence here. It may be quite light at high altitude when it is too dark for safe landing on the ground. In a glider equipped for night flight, a pilot has been known to make his final glide into a lighted airport. Most pilots would feel this to be rather a chancy procedure. But if a World Record were at stake—!

29. Make it a habit at the top of each climb to assess the soaring weather ahead with a view to changing course slightly if this promises better lift. Sometimes one can see trouble-spots far ahead and plan the best route around them.

30. Try often. Each flight increases piloting skills and experience. Not many have earned the Distance Diamond on the first attempt. If it were that easy, the Diamond would not have the significance which it undoubtedly possesses.

TEAM CROSS-COUNTRY

This is a topic about which there is much disagreement among sailplane pilots at the time of writing. The question which remains open, or at least unproven, is whether two or more pilots using concepts of teamwork can fly farther and faster than if they flew singly. Suggesting the value of the team-flying concept is a world record 544 mile flight across Germany and France on June 2, 1963. Also, the Polish team has used team techniques effectively in the World Championships held at Lasham, Great Britain. No group in this country has yet undertaken comparative test flights to determine the worth of team flying, or made a systematic study of what tactics should be used— or if this has been done, the results have never been published. It is high time the matter was settled.

Here is one approach to team flying which, in view of the state of the art, is neither the only, nor likely the best strategy. Two (or more) gliders fly line abreast between thermals, far enough apart so they are unlikely to contact the same thermal. This spacing should nearly double the number of thermals contacted by the team, allowing a more selective policy in their use and, in a weak area, increasing the probability of remaining airborne. When one pilot locates, checks, and approves a thermal, he calls the other to join him. The pilot who reaches the top first departs at an angle to the course line to regain the cruise spacing, while the other leaves on course. The cycle then repeats.

The gliders should be of roughly similar performance. Radio communication is highly desirable, but should be extremely terse. The team should have a captain, responsible for decision-making.

Apart from possible benefits on the world competitive scene, team flying provides a splendid way for clubs to introduce less-experienced members to the pleasures of cross-country flying. The senior member in experience can act as team captain, the others learning and enjoying, and if the guidance is sound the flight will be safer and possibly longer than it would otherwise have been.

While soaring pilots tend to be lone eagles, there are many who would enjoy flying their cross-countries with a friend or a group. Even if all the other benefits of team flying prove out badly, the fun of going together rather than separately is quite appealing.

AFTER AN OFF-FIELD LANDING

After landing off-field there may be problems of safety both for the glider and the pilot. The nature of the problems depends on both geography and weather. So diverse are conditions in this country that the purpose of this brief discussion is to call attention to the need for planning rather than to offer solutions which the pilot is in a better position to work out for himself.

Consider first the needs of the pilot. In populous areas he may have no other need than what remains of the food and water which he had for refreshment during the flight. At the other extreme, in the wilderness areas of the U.S. and Canada, the pilot might need most of the basic Air Force survival kit. A desert landing in summer calls for water (minimum, 2 qts; a gallon is better), salt tablets, food, signaling mirror, two-way radio, flashlight and spare batteries for a night-time walk-out, snake-bite kit, "Space Blanket," and possibly other items.

Landing in the desert is a rather special situation, but so many pilots from other parts of the country are attracted by this magnificent soaring that some further comment is warranted. Before a desert flight, arrangements should be made for an air search beginning the following dawn if the pilot is not heard from before then. During the flight, good 2-way radio contact with a crew car is a big safety factor. If the glider outruns the automobile, as is often the case, the pilot can make en route position reports to FAA Flight Service Stations which would be very helpful later in case of an air search.

During the flight the pilot should be taking into consideration the possibility of having to land, and try to stay reasonably near a well-travelled highway. Keep the hike short. After landing, the pilot ought to stay with the glider until the sun is low and the desert starts cooling, meanwhile resting quietly in the shade of the wing and replenishing the body's water and salt as available supplies permit. If a walk-out appears practical it should not be commenced before dusk. If in doubt, stay with the glider because an air search will find the glider quite easily when a hiker wandering in the scrub would be pretty hard to locate.

Good soaring days often end in local thunderstorms almost anywhere in the country. As a minimum, the pilot should take along a tie-down kit and glider disassembly tools. If conditions are threatening, the pilot should stay with the glider if at all possible until the weather improves, as it often does before dark. He can provide maximum protection from high winds by sitting in the cockpit, keeping spoilers open (or flaps up), the wheel brake set and the stick forward.

If it is essential for the pilot to leave the glider under threatening conditions, he should use all his ingenuity to make it as secure as possible. If he has help, he can remove a wing. If not, he may be able to reduce the wing's angle of attack by putting the wheel in a depression or the tail on a high spot. Gliders with nose skids can be made quite secure by putting rocks in the nose until the skid rests on the ground. The best use should be made of the tie-down kit, always trying to neutralize the lift of the wing or to prevent the wind from getting under a high wing and flipping the glider over. The pilot's parachute may be lashed to an upwind wingtip for this purpose.

A final thought: try to avoid landing in a field occupied by livestock. Animals have been known to trample and even to chew upon a sailplane, while a bull can deal harshly with the pilot.

Dart — photo by Alex Aldott

14. USING OTHER LIFT SOURCES

RIDGE AND SLOPE SOARING

Winds which are deflected upward by all manner of terrain features (mountains, cliffs, hills etc.) provide a special type of lift quite different from thermals. The pattern of the air currents is determined by the force and direction of the wind and the shape of the obstacles which it encounters. In general, there is lift upwind of a hill and sink along the lee slopes. Wherever the contours of the earth change direction too abruptly for the wind to follow smoothly there will be areas of turbulence which can be hazardous for gliders. An example of this is the over-curl at the lee side of a steep ridge. If a pilot must fly through such areas he should maintain *plenty* of reserve speed and stay well away from the grasping hillside.

The technique of ridge soaring is to fly parallel to the upwind slope, crabbing into the wind as necessary. The trusty variometer will show the areas where lift is best. When the glider reaches the end of the lift, the pilot reverses direction and retraces his path along the slope. The proper indicated airspeed depends on how close the glider is to the slope. At a comfortable distance away from the slope or above it, the speed for minimum sink is most efficient. As one goes close to the slope, one should speed up in order to have a reserve of control power and wing lift; at best **glide** speed, control is good and the penalty in higher sink rate is very small.

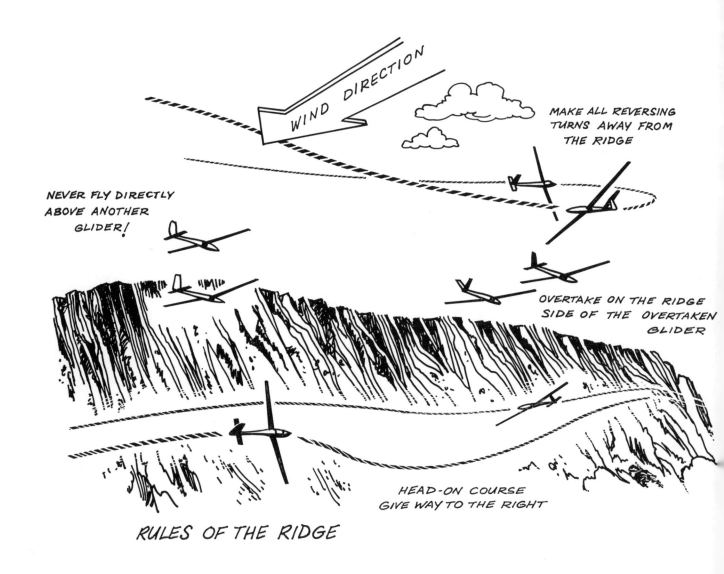

WIND DIRECTION

MAKE ALL REVERSING TURNS AWAY FROM THE RIDGE

NEVER FLY DIRECTLY ABOVE ANOTHER GLIDER!

OVERTAKE ON THE RIDGE SIDE OF THE OVERTAKEN GLIDER

HEAD-ON COURSE GIVE WAY TO THE RIGHT

RULES OF THE RIDGE

Four *Rules of the Ridge* govern nearly all slope soaring:

1. Make all reversing turns away from the ridge, i.e., into the wind. A downwind turn toward the slope is liable to force the glider into the hillside.

2. Never fly directly above or beneath another glider. The pilot above cannot see the lower glider and might nose down into it.

3. Gliders approaching each other head-on give way to the right.

4. An overtaking glider passes between the slope and the overtaken craft. With the slope on the left, this means passing to the left, contrary to the rules of general aviation. This is a necessary deviation from general practice to avoid having the overtaken glider turn in front of the other.

These rules are followed almost everywhere. There are also special local rules (which may even modify the four basic rules) at some ridge soaring sites where schools and clubs operate. These may be made necessary by the location of the landing strip or the presence of areas of sink or turbulence due to the contours of the terrain, or for other reasons. A pilot new to such a soaring site will be properly briefed before take-off.

Slope soaring at a well-organized operation is a delightful and a safe way to spend an afternoon, and offers the potential reward of earning the five hour duration leg for the Silver or Gold FAI Badge.

WAVE SOARING

Mountain waves, lee waves, standing waves, or just plain waves are all the same thing. They are the source of lift for all the present altitude records, for some cross-country flights at speeds greater than is so far possible by thermaling, and for year-around pleasure soaring when conditions are favorable.

The ridge lift directly over a mountain range can only carry a glider a few hundred feet higher than the crests. By a miracle of the atmosphere, the same air flowing through the first lee wave may take a glider up to ten times the height of the summits above the adjacent valley. This may someday be proved a serious understatement of the potential of wave lift; as far as present knowledge goes, it is not an exaggeration.

Perhaps the simplest way to visualize a lee wave is to compare it with the more familiar behavior of water in a river. Imagine a stream with a smooth surface and a flat sandy bottom; then suppose a log were anchored to the bottom, across the stream. The water would flow up over the log, comparable to the ridge lift over a mountain range. It would then flow down, making a trough, then up, down, up, down, many times, making a diminishing succession of crests and troughs. This system of lee waves would hold its position relative to the stream bed and the log, even as the water flows through it, from which circumstance the name "standing wave" is derived. Atmospheric waves are similar.

When a wind blows across two or more parallel mountain ranges, the secondary and later ridges also create waves. These waves may amplify or cancel out the primary wave, depending on their relative wavelengths, amplitudes and phase (timing).

Under the first lee wave the wind swirls down and up again in a horizontal whirl called the rotor. Under succeeding waves the rotor action diminishes rapidly, and may even be absent. The turbulence under the first wave may be extremely violent, comparable to that found in severe thunderstorms, and is in startling contrast to the silky smoothness of the wave lift. The top of the rotor is usually about even with the crests of the mountains generating the wave. The bottom of the rotor may reach to the ground, where it will produce strong and highly variable surface winds and extreme gustiness. Several airports are located where rotor action occurs right down the runway every so often. A landing then calls for extra speed, close to the glider's maximum maneuvering speed, maintained until the wheel is on the ground. Such a landing is beyond a doubt one of soaring's more exciting moments, one calculated to make full use of the pilot's skills and faculties.

The existence of wave clouds and the amount of cloud cover depend on the humidity of the air aloft, and has nothing to do with the process of wave formation. Waves may be completely hidden in a solid overcast or be equally well concealed in a clear blue sky. The situation most helpful to the glider pilot is when the air is just moist enough to provide clouds which map the geography of the wave system.

The characteristic wave cloud is formed

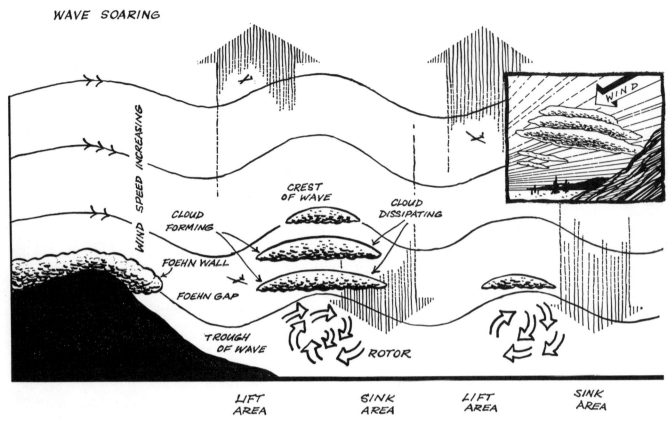

CREST OF WAVE

CLOUD FORMING

CLOUD DISSIPATING

WIND

WIND SPEED INCREASING

FOEHN WALL

FOEHN GAP

TROUGH OF WAVE

ROTOR

LIFT AREA

SINK AREA

LIFT AREA

SINK AREA

THE WIND IS INCREASINGLY STRONGER WITH INCREASING ALTITUDE THEREFORE GLIDERS MUST CRAB MORE AND MORE INTO WIND AND INCREASE SPEED IN ORDER TO STAY IN AREA OF LIFT

when the rising air downwind of the wave trough is cooled by expansion to the dew point and moisture condenses. The cloud thus formed moves up and over the crest of the wave and down the other side until compression warming evaporates it. The cross-section of the resulting cloud is that of a lens, from which it gets the name "lenticular," or "lennie" in soaring slang. A lenticular is also called a standing wave cloud, after its other important characteristic.

The band of clear air which often appears between the mountains and the first lenticular cloud is called the Foehn gap. (The *oeh* vowel sound is pronounced like the "u" in *urn*.) The gap is the result of compression warming of the air sliding down the mountainside, which

evaporates any clouds that covered the crests. The significant fact which a pilot should remember is the startling rapidity with which the Foehn gap can fill with clouds and disappear. So can the similar gaps between successive downwind lenticulars.

The Weather Bureau can forecast conditions favorable for wave formation with considerable accuracy, their winds aloft and radiosonde temperature and humidity soundings providing the necessary data. The vertical temperature distribution most favorable to wave formation is a layer of stable air (or even an inversion) around mountaintop altitude, with less stable air both above and below it. The wind across the ridge should be at least 20 mph, or even faster if the wind direction is oblique to the mountain range. The wind should increase rapidly with altitude above the crest level. For recording existing wave cloud patterns, our satellite cloud pictures are absolutely magnificent. Alas, they are not available quickly enough to be much practical help to sailplane pilots except as study material for planning future wave flights.

Waves, both dry ones and those marked by clouds, occur in every month of the year. Both kinds of waves were encountered by pilots in the 1966 National Championships at Reno in the month of July. However, the frequency of waves is least in summer, greater in spring and fall, and most frequent in the winter.

The technique of wave flight is quite simple once the geography of the wave system is understood. Usually the glider is towed into the smooth lift of the wave, avoiding the rotor area if this is possible. Sometimes, in order to have a low release point, a pilot will release in the upwind side of the rotor, working the lift and fighting the turbulence until he climbs into the wave. Rotor or wave lift are both worked in the manner of slope lift, by sweeps across the wind. As guidance, the pilot must keep track of his position over the ground. The line of best lift may be quite narrow, but moves very little, and then only as the entire wave system changes. In combating rotor turbulence, the pilot cannot "chase the airspeed," which shoots up and down rapidly. The best he can do is try to keep the attitude of the glider as steady as he can, use the controls smoothly to minimize maneuvering loads, and try to keep the *average* airspeed reading somewhere near best glide speed. When the glider emerges into the smooth wave lift, the speed should be reduced to minimum sink and trimmed if there is a trimmer.

As the climb continues, the need to shuttle back and forth diminishes until finally the wind may become strong enough to fly the glider straight into it, remaining stationary in rela-

tion to the earth. Climbing higher, it may become necessary to speed up to keep from being blown back into a lennie or at least back from the area of best lift.

So long as the rate of climb is satisfactory there is no reason for moving about, but when it drops off the pilot should explore the area of lift. The best rate of climb will usually be found in the lee of the highest peak in the range that is generating the wave. Often this spot will be indicated by the shape of the lenticular cloud.

Cross-country flights using wave lift are not uncommon. The technique used depends on which way the pilot wants to go in relation to the wind. No one would plan a cross-country against the wind, but triangles and goal-and-return flights have been completed by going upwind from wave to wave. When diving from the high point of one wave through the sink of the next upwind wave, the rate of sink is staggering, and the time spent regaining the altitude is proportionately great. The only good feature of moving against the wind is that each successive wave should be stronger than the last, up to the first lee wave.

The greatest speed in cross-country flight is offered by the downwind course through a series of waves. When diving through the area of strongest sink (at the speed-to-fly, if you dare) the ground speed may be more than 300 mph, and the high *true* airspeed requires the pilot to be alert to spot the next "up" and to whirl around into the wind for the next climb.

A slower, and perhaps more reliable way to go cross-country is cross-wind, along the wave. A pilot can declare a distance or a goal-and-return flight, and if conditions remain favorable, can stay in the same wave for the entire flight. Any of our long chains of mountains, East or West, will occasionally set up waves which offer spectacular possibilities.

Obviously, wave flights can carry a pilot into a hostile environment where it would be suicidal to venture without special training, clothing and equipment. The Soaring Society of America has arranged with the Air Force for a course of training making use of the AF high-altitude chambers. SSA is now urging that no pilot be permitted to fly to altitudes at which oxygen is required without proof of formal instruction in altitude oxygen equipment and procedures. The reading of this or any other book doesn't even come close to the benefit derived from the Air Force high altitude indoctrination course. Don't miss it; the opportunity might not always be there.

Not all wave flying involves high altitudes and the need for supplemental oxygen. There are many soaring sites with nearby hills and mountains where modest soarable waves can be found at any season. Waves farther downwind than the first or second offer smoother flying and pleasure soaring of top caliber. Soarable waves often appear when the wind strengthens enough to break up the thermals, increasing the number of soarable days in the year.

LESS USED SOURCES OF LIFT

The early morning sun strikes the east-facing slope of a mountain squarely enough to warm the entire slope before the valley floor reaches triggering temperature. The air close to the mountainside is warmed and moves up the slope in a thin layer. If the lift reaches condensation level, cumulus will form, often appearing as a little cloud cap over the mountain. This form of thermal lift, not restricted to the early hours, is quite different from the usual thermal; it is called "anabatic." It extends out from the slope from 100 to 300 feet, and is worked in the same manner and with the same cautions as ordinary slope winds.

A special use of anabatic lift (a use which it shares with lee waves) is to make possible an early start for a cross-country flight. In order to have a low release point, the pilot releases from aero tow as near the bottom of the mountain as he thinks the lift will support him. He then laboriously works his way up to the summit, where he remains until he feels the time has come to push off on course toward the nearest likely thermal source. This should be all planned out ahead of time. With good judgment (good luck is also to be desired), a high mountain and a flat-gliding sailplane, this technique can add many miles to the day's flight.

Anabatic winds in reverse, called catabatic or drainage winds, occur when the shaded side of a mountain loses heat by radiation and then cools the air in contact with it. This localized downslope wind can reach a velocity of 20 to 30 mph, accelerating as it moves downward. Then it moves out over the still sunny valley floor where it pushes beneath the air still being warmed by the afternoon sunshine, boosting it upward like a tiny cold front. It is a good idea to leave the east-facing slopes when the lift on them begins to weaken and seek out these valley thermals or hunt up some westward facing slopes.

* * *

As sources of lift, cold fronts and the squall lines that form 50 to 100 miles ahead of them are for the experienced and adventurous, not for novices. An advancing cold front pushes under the warmer moist air, lifting it and triggering lines of thunderstorms. Very strong lift will be found beneath the leading edge of these storms. The pilot can, by his position relative to the storm, to a certain degree choose the strength of his lift and the ruggedness of his flying conditions. Weaker conditions are found farther ahead of the storm, and more strenuous ones back under the edge of the Cu-nim. Forces can be very great, and there is always a chance of being drawn up into the thunderhead.

* * *

A convergence or shear line (the distinction is a niggling one) is an area where two bodies of air which are moving relative to each other, meet. The terms are used for smaller, more local phenomena than the great fronts we see on the weather map of the U.S., but they are essentially similar. The lift of a convergence zone is usually rather narrow, and if one of the air masses is moist it may be marked by a line of small cumulus. An example of a convergence is the Elsinore, California "Smog Front." Here the smog-laden air from the Pomona Valley meets the cooler moist air coming up the Elsinore Valley from the sea. The front is too short to take a glider any significant distance, but it provides a lot of fun for local soaring.

               ❀   ❀   ❀

Sea breeze fronts fit the same description as shears and convergences. About mid-morning the warming land mass provides rising air which is replaced by cool air moving in from the ocean. This is the familiar sea breeze that keeps the beach resorts cool in summer. From the air, the sea breeze front can often be seen because of the haze in the moist sea air; it may also be marked by a line of small cumulus.

Sea breeze fronts are found along any of our coastlines whenever they are not broken up by stronger winds. They have not as yet provided the lift for any long flights, but are fine for local soaring, and might possibly support a five-hour duration flight.

15. MOUNTAIN SOARING

Our country's mountain ranges offer conditions where a pilot can experience to the full the joy of soaring. Here, all the principal forms of lift may be found—thermal, wave, anabatic and slope winds. The scenery is usually magnificent. Soaring birds share the sport with sailplane pilots. The eagle circling at 15,000 feet at the top of a thermal is obviously there just for the fun of it, since he does his meal hunting much closer to the ground. Here the soaring human also finds freedom from earthly cares, exhilaration and inspiration.

When mountain lift is strong, the descending currents are proportionately vigorous; the variometer is often pegged—up or down. There is a potential hazard in rates of sink greater than a thousand feet per minute. A pilot who has not thought much about how air flows over mountainous terrain could easily blunder into trouble.

"PASS FRIEND"

MOUNTAIN SOARING

"CURL OVER"
FORCES GLIDER TO
TURN AWAY FROM
RIDGE CROSSING ATTEMPT

Lift and sink follow logical patterns everywhere, but in the mountains the relationship of cause and effect are more obvious to a sailplane pilot than over level country. The shape of the terrain in its relation to the wind, the heating of the sun-facing slopes, the steep valley rising to a notch between peaks where a venturi effect magnifies the wind and lift, are all predictable conditions. They have their opposites on the lee sides and shaded slopes where the pilot can be fairly sure of descending like the proverbial streamlined brick. Areas of overcurl or severe turbulence can be inferred from abrupt changes in angle between the terrain and the wind direction. It is a parallel situation to the behavior of the air over the top of a wing, where the wind follows the wing smoothly up to a certain angle, then breaks away in a turbulent wake. When a steep ridge

is to be approached from the downwind side, it must be at high speed and from an altitude substantially above the ridge. The pilot may have to turn and run if at the last minute the passage looks doubtful—the trees along the crest can grow magically taller in just a few seconds and seem to reach out with their branches to grab the glider and its pilot. It's almost spooky.

Approaching the ridge from the upwind side is spooky in just the opposite way. Often one can approach obliquely (to make it easy to turn away) at an altitude a hundred or even two hundred feet below the ridge, and at the last minute the mountain mysteriously sinks out of the way, as if to say "Pass, Friend."

• • •

Thermals may be triggered anywhere on a sunny slope. When the wind is flowing up the slope, the thermal moves with it and may pass close to the crest, or at a little distance out from it. A pilot who is slope soaring will do well to prospect for thermals a little way upwind of the ridge; if successful, it will probably take him far higher than the slope lift could.

In the mountains, flying at minimum sink speed is indicated only when well away from the surface of the slope. The fact that the best rate of climb may be found when only a wingspan or less from the slope tempts the pilot to move in really close. Yielding to this temptation demands of the pilot extreme vigilance and increased airspeed to provide lots of aileron control and a reserve of lift for pulling away from the slope. Experienced pilots are also careful to stay out of box canyons and narrow valleys where limited turning room coupled with heavy sink or turbulence could produce big trouble.

*　*　*

To make cross-country progress in the mountains it is often necessary to hurry across areas where heavy sink can be anticipated. The technique is to accelerate to high speed before leaving the rising air, and then to dash out into the sink. Waiting to accelerate until the vario has turned down exacts a heavier penalty in altitude. A knowledge of speeds-to-fly is essential, and the airspeed should be adjusted as necessary all the way across the area of sink in order to achieve the *least bad* glide angle under the circumstances. Turbulence should be considered when deciding how fast to fly; after all, *some* glide angle may be sacrificed to keep the glider in one piece.

In the mountains good places to land are scarcer than tricycles on the freeway. To land safely, a pilot usually has to come away from the mountains to a valley where there is enough level and cleared land for a sailplane. This means he must always have an escape route planned. When conditions change and the altimeter starts unwinding, tarry not; move out of the mountains. Gliders are expensive.

If the pilot miscalculates and is forced down in hostile terrain, there are really only two rules to remember: land into the wind, and do not stall. Land at low speed, yes, but land it flying, not mushing down. If this is done, the pilot's injuries will probably be limited to the sensitive area of the pocketbook.

The reader should appreciate that a book of instruction such as this *must* tell about the problems to be avoided. Consequently there is an atmosphere of hazard which is entirely out of proportion to the realities of soaring. This is especially true when discussing mountain soaring, which on the whole is easy, safe and delightful if the pilot exercises a degree of informed prudence.

16. TRANSITION TO HIGH PERFORMANCE SAILPLANES

High performance gliders in general are no more difficult to fly than are those of lesser L/D, or training types (some are even easier), but they *are* different. Before taking off in a more advanced single seater, a pilot will benefit from some dual instruction in a two-place machine of similar characteristics. The training should include: steep turns, the series of stalls, spins, speed control while changing angle of descent, and accuracy landings.

The stall behavior of a few high performance gliders is rather abrupt, with a tendency for a wing to drop and a spin to develop. In small rough thermals, when the pilot is banking steeply, this abrupt stall may be frequent, and is countered with relaxed back stick followed by a coordinated return to the thermaling angle of bank without losing position in the thermal. In the traffic pattern, an abrupt stall characteristic underlines the need for holding normal pattern airspeed as an absolute minimum.

At the present time the majority of high performance sailplanes have both spoilers and camber-changing flaps with limited travel up and down. The flaps are raised for high-speed cruising and lowered for thermaling. On entering the traffic pattern the flaps are lowered to the landing setting and remain in this position. The spoilers and elevators are then used together for controlling the angle of descent exactly as in a trainer.

Before actually flying any entirely strange glider, the manufacturer's flight instructions should be studied carefully. There should be detailed recommendations for all areas of flight, and also a performance curve. Unfortunately, the manual is not likely to include speeds-to-fly, which the pilot will have to compute for himself; this should not be needed on a first flight.

If a pilot is available who is familiar with the behavior of the new glider, he should be consulted. Finally, the transitioning pilot would do well to spend some time in the cockpit familiarizing himself with the location and functioning of the controls and instruments. Power pilots have been known, in moments of stress, to push the wrong lever when in an unfamiliar aircraft, a possibility which even glider pilots should recognize and guard against. The Air Force has a "good thing" in requiring a pilot to pass a blindfold test in the cockpit.

In the absence of good climbing conditions, a high tow should be taken for the first flight in a new type glider. An altitude of 4000' AGL will give the pilot plenty of time to get acquainted with the craft before coming in for a landing. First, a few coordination exercises should be done to feel out the balance of rudder and ailerons. Then some steep turns are in order, followed by the stall series both with and without spoilers; indications of the approaching stall and the airspeed at the stall should be noted. Last, a final approach should be simulated, practicing changing the angle of descent keeping the airspeed constant. The wheel should be lowered during this maneuver if it is the retractable variety. If there is no landing-gear warning signal, a handkerchief may be tied to the spoiler handle for a reminder. If the pilot *owns* the retractable gem he should install a warning signal without delay.

When the pilot is satisfied that he has the feel of the new glider, he is ready to enter the traffic pattern for a landing. He can change the pattern altitude if this seems necessary. A few sailplanes have only three glide angles: flat, flatter and flattest. For such gliders a lower pattern is indicated. The landing spot should be about a third of the way down the field to provide for errors of over or undershooting.

As a final suggestion, some local flying is in order before the pilot goes cross-country to rewrite the record book. Flying the glider should be as automatic as possible, to allow the pilot to give his full attention to the in-flight decision-making on which the success of any cross-country depends.

At this stage in the story, the lucky pilot should be up to his ears in the joy of soaring.

USING HIGH-DRAG FLAPS

At the time of writing the HP series and the BG's are the only U.S. built gliders using high-drag flaps without supplementary spoilers or dive brakes. More are likely to appear, since this style flap has been approved "in principle" by the gliding committee (C.I.V.V.) of the FAI for Standard Class Competition beginning with the 1972 World Championships. These gliders handle differently in some ways from those equipped with spoilers.

A good way to get acquainted with the differences is to have some dual instruction in a similarly equipped power plane such as the Cessna 150 or the Supercub. The maneuvers described below should be practiced using a power setting just over idling to simulate the behavior of a sailplane.

The basic difference between spoilers and these flaps is that spoilers decrease a wing's lift whereas flaps increase lift. (Both increase the drag.) What this means to the pilot is that—assuming no change in pitch attitude—opening spoilers causes the glider to sink while decelerating, whereas lowering the flaps causes

it to balloon, up to the moment when it runs out of flying speed. Looking at the reverse actions, again assuming that the pilot makes no compensating change in pitch attitude, the effect of closing the spoilers is to check the rate of descent while accelerating, whereas raising the flaps will increase the rate of descent. The glider with spoilers open stalls faster than when they are closed. Flaps have the opposite effect of reducing the stalling speed. Raising the flaps when below the flaps-up stalling speed produces an immediate stall. These are the fundamentals underlying the proper techniques for flying either type glider.

Regarding take-off flap settings, the manufacturer's recommendations should be followed. These usually suggest a small amount of down flap (5 or 10 degrees) which will increase lift slightly without unduly increasing drag.

Up to the present, the plain hinged flap has been difficult to lower at high speed, so when a rapid let-down is planned the flaps should be lowered before the glider is nosed down. In cloud flying, flaps should be put down at the first sign of a speed buildup that the pilot is unable to control. Perhaps future flapped gliders will have enough mechanical advantage in the flap control system to lower the flaps at red-line speed. We shall see.

The use of flaps in the traffic pattern is similar to spoilers. Stick and flap control are coordinated to maintain a constant airspeed while varying the angle of descent. "Practice makes perfect," it says here. When practicing, begin with very deliberate changes, being careful not to move one control without the other.

Pattern airspeed for flapped gliders should be based on the *flaps-up* stalling speed. The rule is the same as for spoiler-type sailplanes: 50% above the stalling speed plus half the estimated wind velocity, maintained scrupulously up to the flaring out. If this speed is maintained, flaps may be used freely to control glide angle in either direction without fear of stalling. Flaps down, nose down; flaps up, nose up.

On final approach, the technique of aiming the glider at the flare-out point is the same as with spoilers. The flaring out process is the point where a transitioning pilot must learn a new skill—how to make a full-flap landing without ballooning and then dropping it in. Learning by easy stages is the way to do it. The first few landings should be made without any change in flap setting after the flare-out is begun. The glider's behavior will be the same as with spoilers, except perhaps for a noticeable reduction of speed at touchdown.

The next step is to start lowering the flaps further as the flare-out progresses. The nose will be raised much more slowly since lowering the flaps increases the lift and checks the rate of descent. However, the glider is touched down in the usual level flight attitude. Over a series of landings the amount of flaps used may be increased as the pilot gains confidence in his ability to avoid ballooning and to follow a normal path of rounding out the descent.

The post-graduate stage in the use of flaps is directed toward the short-field landing after an approach over an obstacle such as a row of trees. On final approach the glider is aimed so as to clear the trees by a safe margin, is then nosed down steeply as the flaps are lowered fully, and is then flared out and landed. Full pattern airspeed is a *must* up to the flare-out in order to be able to check the very steep descent. The drag of the flaps lowered 90 degrees is so great that as the round-out is completed the glider will be ready to land after little or no float. It is *through flying*, so refrain from flaring out ten feet up. This maneuver also should be approached by easy stages. Its worth lies in the unmatched capability to squeeze into a small field and touch down at minimum speed, with a correspondingly short rollout. Not for beginners.

When checking out solo in a glider with high-drag flaps an even higher tow is suggested. In addition to the usual familiarization maneuvers, the pilot will want to simulate a few flare-outs to learn how rapidly the glider loses airspeed with different flap settings. In landing, the prime object is to avoid ballooning and dropping it in.

17. SAFETY

COMPLEXITY OF MISHAPS

The safety record of soaring compares very favorably with that of any other activity involving men in motion. However, when a man is in motion there is always a chance that the motion will be interrupted with unhappy results. It is even so with soaring.

If we could lay the blame for each accident upon a single cause, accidents would be easier to analyse and perhaps to avoid. Very often, however, a chain of contributory events precedes a mishap. Consider the following imaginary but typical sequence of events:

1. A pilot has an irresistible urge to show off his fancied aerobatic ability.
2. He flies a WW II surplus glider with a low red-line speed.
3. His aerobatics end in an excessive dive.
4. He pulls out too fast, overstressing the structure.
5. He does not wear a parachute.

The preceding example points up the difficulty in helping a pilot to fly a glider safely. One must perforce discuss the leading causes of accidents singly, yet there are usually other factors involved, often in the mind of the pilot.

PSYCHOLOGICAL AND EMOTIONAL FACTORS

In the hypothetical accident of the preceding section, the report of the official investigator would probably say "structural failure" and include a description of the pilot's actions that caused the failure. The real cause, without which there would have been no accident, is the immature desire on the part of the pilot to show off. A secondary cause, also mental, is the pilot's belief that he is adequately trained to perform aerobatics when in fact he is not.

Consider the case of a pilot who knows perfectly well that the rules at his home airport specify a traffic pattern entry at 1000 feet AGL and require that he stay in the pattern until safely on the ground. He encounters lift, circles in it and is blown downwind of the field. The lift becomes sink, he can't penetrate back, and damages the glider while making an off-field landing. That is pilot error, not in flying ability but in self-discipline.

Then there is the pilot who lands off-field a couple of miles away from the pattern entry point. On being challenged for his reason for being so low so far away, he sheepishly replies "I got in strong sink." That pilot may fly a glider well enough to pass an FAA flight test, but his poor planning shows a lack of understanding of the convective cycle (if there's lift, there is also sink.) and ignorance of the requirements of motorless flight. There may also be an over-confident "it can't happen to me" psychology.

An emotional factor enters into many accidents. A person suddenly faced with a situation that he has not been trained to handle, or does not expect, may go into a state of shock and behave quite irrationally. For another hypothetical example, a pilot of a high performance glider with very effective spoilers is on final approach. He sees another glider on the field precisely where he expects to touch down. Although there is room to land short with full spoilers, to overfly the glider with closed spoilers, or to pass to one side, the pilot noses down, flies the glider onto the ground at excessive speed and rolls briskly into the other machine. When asked why he didn't slip to one side and pass safely, he replies "I tried to, but the controls wouldn't move. The glider wouldn't turn." Examination shows all controls functioning normally.

Another pilot who lets himself get low far from the airport suddenly awakes to the situation and concludes he can't make it back to the field. As panicked as a fleeing rabbit, he speeds up to 70 mph, flies past a safe off-field landing site, and crashes into a tree while still doing 70 mph, a mere hundred yards from the airport boundary. He does not recognize that he was upwind of the airport and can fly well beyond it at best glide speed. He even has enough speed to float onto the airport for a safe landing, but his state of shock prevents him from recognizing the fact.

These pilots do not err in flying technique, they err in a failure to understand and be guided by the basic principles of soaring. As a consequence, perfectly normal and controllable situations appear to them as dangerous crises. Fear and shock then account for the illogical behavior.

Better training for pilots is the obvious and pat answer to this situation, and it has merit. But the mental attitude of the pilot is also important. A *pilot* is one who plans ahead and is concerned with the various possible emergencies, crossing the bridges mentally before he comes to them. A *good* pilot is not just a blithe unthinking hedonist.

THE PLACARD

Every glider carries an operations limitation placard. It is there to protect the pilot (so far as it can) from accidents caused by improper weight or balance or by excessive speed.

The glider is engineered to withstand certain assumed stresses at its design *maximum gross weight*. Overloading the craft reduces permissible "G" loads, maximum speed, and safety factors. The word for overloading is "don't".

Balance means fore and aft placement of the center of gravity. When the CG is outside permissible limits, control at low speed is impaired and spin characteristics are adversely affected. In fact, spin recovery may even become impossible. Since a glider is normally thermaled close to the stall, observance of CG limits is absolutely essential for safety. The placard states the CG requirements in terms of maximum and minimum weights of pilot and passenger.

The placard states the safe *maximum glide speed* and the *maximum aero tow* and *ground launch speeds*. All deserve the utmost respect. The maximum glide speed (red-line speed) needs some explanation because of the possible inference that no harm can come to the glider so long as this speed is not exceeded. This is far from the case. Below red-line speed, heavy gusts or maneuvering loads can tear the wings off a glider.

Gust is a four letter word for the phenomena of turbulence, all the external forces which a passenger describes unprofessionally as "bumps." When a glider is flown below its design *maneuvering speed* gusts will not do structural damage; above that speed, the pilot had better take care. If he insists upon flying above maneuvering speed in rough air, and most pilots do upon occasion, an accelerometer will help him judge what speed is safe.° Three-G bumps are hard enough. The

limit load factor, a little over five-G in most gliders, should not be approached because the next bump may be harder than the last, or may coincide with a maneuvering load, adding up to an *over*-load. The *ultimate load factor* is not the guiding value, as serious damage can occur before the structure fails completely. When a glider has no accelerometer, the pilot can use his own comfort as a warning signal. Uncomfortable bumps are a not-so-gentle hint to slow down. If the pilot happens to be one of those people insensitive to discomfort, the warning comes when, despite the restraints of the belt and shoulder straps, he lifts clear of the seat or bangs his head on the canopy— or when his eyeglasses fall off, as one eminent pilot suggests.

Maneuvering loads are those imposed on the glider by use of the controls. The *maximum maneuvering speed* is the fastest at which full and abrupt movement of the controls is possible without structural damage. This speed varies with different types of gliders, but is generally within the range of 1.7 to 2.5 times stalling speed. Maximum maneuvering speed is important in aerobatics, where smooth and well-judged use of the controls is especially desirable since the glider might be subjected simultaneously to gust and maneuvering loads.

Summing up, a glider can withstand almost any stress below the maximum maneuvering speed, simply because the wing will stall, limiting the stress. Beyond this speed, up to the red line, control deflections should be applied smoothly, i.e., *slowly*. Any uncomfortable bump is a signal to slow down.

FLUTTER

Flutter is a phenomenon of high speed that is little spoken of or thought about by glider pilots. It is a rapid oscillation of some part of the glider that builds up quickly and can easily cause structural failure before the pilot can react to take any corrective action. Glider de-

---

°An accelerometer should not be installed in a shock-mounted instrument panel. The shock absorbing mounting would absorb what the accelerometer is supposed to record.

signers do take flutter into consideration, but "keep their fingers crossed" because it can be caused by factors outside their control. Flutter below red-line speed can be caused by looseness in control cables, connections, hinges, or play in the wing or empennage attachments, or even by the pilot's action. As an example, a pilot who was gliding straight ahead at high speed took his feet off the rudder pedals to rest his weary legs by a change of position. The fuselage started to shake like a wet puppy, but stopped when he put his feet back on the pedals. By a miracle a safe landing was made. Inspection showed that the rear of the fuselage had almost parted company from the rest of the glider.

EXAMPLE OF FLUTTER

An interesting and puzzling fact about flutter is that the triggering speed is a *true* rather than an indicated airspeed. The implication of this strange fact is that at high altitude, where TAS is far higher than IAS, the speed limit should be the true airspeed given on the placard. In the absence of a speed computer and free-air thermometer, the pilot can mentally deduct 2% per thousand feet ASL from the placard maximum to find the safe indicated red-line speed.

AEROBATICS

The general run of gliders is not particularly well adapted to aerobatics. Naturally there have to be exceptions, as there are gliders that were expressly designed for stunt flying.

Ignoring these, since few pilots ever see such machines, let's consider why the average glider is a poor thing for the livelier aerobatics. Bearing in mind the probability of exceptions to all the following statements, let us proceed:

1. Compared with aerobatic powered planes, the rate of roll of a glider would try the patience of a saint. For example, in the second half of a slow roll the glider will slip sideways at a startling rate, imposing side loads on the fin and rudder for which they were not designed. Ever hopeful, the pilot may then enter the maneuver at higher speed, applying full aileron to hasten the roll, and will probably exceed the aileron and wing torsional design limits. If by chance the slow roll is completed without damage to structure, it will be a sloppy caricature of what a slow roll should be. (Do not infer from the above that the first half of the roll is safer or less sloppy, though it might be—slightly.)

2. Glider designers try to hold down the wetted area (square feet of skin) and the weight. As a result of this worthy aspiration, the empennage areas are the *least* that will provide safe control in normal usage. There simply is not enough rudder and elevator control to provide *snap* maneuvers that are really snappy, even when they are at all possible. The glider pilot who aspires to do double upwardly-vertical snap rolls and recover precisely in a normal glide attitude had best stay in bed and dream about it. The common run of sailplanes will refuse. Snap maneuvers in general are pretty hopeless.

3. What is aerobatics without the inverted repertoire? A spineless nothing. Many gliders are specifically restricted against inverted flight, and most of the rest

are so limited in their capability to withstand negative G loads as to preclude most of the inverted repertory. Inverted snap maneuvers, spins and outside loops—forget 'em.

4. Lack of engine power as well as limited control power eliminate such capers as square loops and section rolls. Alas.

5. The Achilles Heel of the sailplane in aerobatic work is at the same time its greatest virtue in soaring: its fantastically low drag. Acceleration when the glider is pointed straight down is of the heart-in-your-throat variety. Maneuvers which put the glider in this attitude must be handled with discretion, but are possible provided the nose does not *stay* down, as in a square loop, and provided the recovery G loads are kept within reason. In this instance, "reason" means about 3½ G's because of the chance that a gust could add to the maneuvering load, putting the total over the limit.

If all the above is true, what is left for the pilot in whose veins the sap is rising? Surprisingly, quite a little. There are loops and barrel rolls. There are Chandelles, Lazy Eights and wing-overs, and there is the spin, if the pilot's bird is spinnable. These maneuvers are a delight for the pilot with a taste for aerobatics, and when properly executed are within the strength limitations of any glider which has unrestricted FAA approval.

If these aerobatics are too tame to satisfy the pilot, his recourse should be to enroll in a school of aerobatics where good strong aerobatic power aircraft and competent instructors can give appropriate treatment to his spring fevers. He is probably more interested in aerobatics than in soaring. In any case, dual instruction is the way to learn aerobatics, not "Stunt Flying Self-Taught."

THUNDERSTORMS

Pilots who plan deliberately to enter Cu-Nims in the U.S., or other countries where thunderstorms are not anemic, should first ponder the following article from the May 1968 issue of *Soaring*, written by Lt. Col. James M. George. Believe. It is "for real."

"If you're planning to enter the weather arena next summer to battle the thunderstorm, you'd better have your seconds ready with the towel, for the odds are stacked against you. Perhaps you've talked with sailplane pilots who have flown unscathed in cu-nim in quest of a Diamond, or you may even have done it yourself. I have. It can be done, and a few successful (or lucky!) penetrations might cause you to wonder if thunderstorm hazards aren't grossly overrated. They aren't.

There are two important features of these cloud factories: drafts and gusts. Updrafts and downdrafts extend from the bottom to the top of the cloud and may have a horizontal extent of four to eight miles. Updrafts of 50 ft./sec. (3000 ft./min.) are not unusual. The maximum vertical speeds of both the updrafts and downdrafts appear near 26,000 feet. Superimposed upon these drafts are gusts extending from 30 to 300 feet in the vertical. While the drafts produce a systematic displacement of the sailplane—in extreme cases as much as 6000 feet either up or down—the gusts cause that violent pitching, rolling, and yawing so discomforting to those of us who have been sucked into a giant, growing cloud.

The resulting turbulence can be found at any altitude, although usually the maximum frequency of the higher-velocity gusts appears near the freezing level. This means that, on the average, the most severe turbulence lies normally between 10,000 and 18,000 feet. But—and there are always but's when it comes to thunderstorms—gust velocities often show an increase up to within 5000 to 10,000 feet of the top of the cloud. For this reason severe turbulence may be distributed over a considerable portion of the cloud. It is important to point out that the most severe turbulence coincides with areas of heavy precipitation, though this is contrary to what was once thought. Staying out of the heaviest rainfall areas will, therefore, reduce the turbulence to some extent.

All your troubles won't end there, however. As you've been taught, clear icing is supposed to give you more trouble than rime and is found most frequently in cumuliform clouds. This is true—only, here's another one of those but's— but without underestimating the danger of thunderstorm ice, it can be said that it is not a particularly serious threat, *normally*. The reason? You're not normally subjected to icing conditions long enough. Icing does exist, though; a "Thunderstorm Project" sailplane (for the USAF) that was spiraling upward within a thunderstorm iced so badly that the pilot lost all use of his elevators. In this case, the sailplane had been subjected to an icing situation for approximately 12 minutes. [Duke Mancuso, who flew his sailplane IFR in conjunction with the work that won him the Tuntland Award in 1959, recommends that the pilot keep moving the controls to keep them from freezing in one position—or, as Duke puts it, "It helps to tremble a lot."—Ed.]

Now, you have heard a lot about thunderstorm hail. Power pilots have encountered hail as high as 31,000 feet, but as a general rule hail is usually found in the middle of the storm or, to put it another way, in the vicinity of the freezing level. Yet another "but" creeps in here, for hail *may* be found at all levels and even outside the thunderstorm cloud, itself. Occasionally it is tossed out the side of the storm cloud, but it may also be borne aloft by strong upcurrents and then spewed out of the anvil top to fall through the clear air. Obviously, you can't ignore the threat of hail when you circumnavigate a grumbling thundercloud. Hail damage to sailplanes is common and costly to re-

pair, even though serious structural damage would be rare. Along with hail, there is the possibility of being struck by lightning. Although at one time it was thought that the chances were slim of lightning in cloud striking or doing much damage, recent evidence in Europe has shown that this was an overoptimistic view.

Lastly, caution in landing around or under a thunderstorm should be adhered to. Gusty surface winds caused by the thunderstorm's downrush can completely ruin the best laid plans for a perfect approach and landing.

This all adds up to one fact: any pilot attempting cu-nim flights must know the risks involved and must make a reasoned decision as to whether they are acceptable on each particular occasion. The potential danger of thunderstorms has been proven beyond a doubt. Take the advice of one who has been there: *never enter them by choice!*"

OFF-FIELD LANDINGS

Off-field landings are a frequent cause of damage to gliders, though seldom of injury to the pilot. Selection of a poor landing area can be the result of postponing the choice until too late. In flight, one should *always* have a suitable landing spot in gliding range, and preferably more than one, since upon closer inspection one of them may prove unsuitable. When a pilot gets low, as he inevitably will, he should confine his search for lift to an area within gliding range of a downwind leg for the field that he chose when higher up. If he finds no more lift, he should fly a proper pattern to give him the best opportunity to pick the spot for touchdown, avoiding irrigation pipes, rocks, high vegetation and other glider breakers.

This procedure requires strength of character, since the human tendency is to keep hunting for lift right down to the ground in an effort to save the flight. This foolish course is promoted by accounts of how this or that contest pilot scored a "save" by ridge soaring along a hangar roof or thermaling over a teacup. But contest pilots, like automobile racing drivers, sometimes take calculated risks; they may be willing to jeopardize their craft in hopes of winning, especially on the last day of a contest. The amount of damage done to gliders in contests bears out this observation, and more power to 'em if the glider owners can afford to pay the repair bills. Personal injury is almost unheard of, since most contest pilots are skillful enough to crash-land in a quarry and walk away from it.

If you were one of these fine and prosperous pilots, you would hardly be reading this book, so readers take heed to the suggestions given elsewhere in this manual in regard to off-field landings, and they will always remain routine incidents of soaring, nothing more.

MID-AIR COLLISION

In theory at least, gliders and the rules for using them should make mid-air collisions as rare as fine pearls in restaurant oysters. Consider the protections given to the soaring pilot:

1. Gliders generally provide excellent pilot visibility.
2. The rule for thermaling in the same direction as others.
3. The rules of ridge soaring.
4. The standardized traffic pattern.

Notwithstanding the above safety factors, there have been too many mid-air collisions, and pilots have been lost thereby. Statistically, the number is negligible, but who wants to be a statistic, even a very small one?

This manual can offer only time-worn suggestions in regard to avoiding mid-air collision:

1. Learn to glance *briefly* at the instruments; absorb their message quickly and look outside the cockpit again "ASAP." Nothing is gained by staring the instruments out of countenance. If possible, use an audio variometer when thermaling.
2. Lubricate well the joints of the pilot's neck—and use them. The effective angular range of the human vision is so very small, especially when focussed on some object such as a checkpoint or a likely-looking cumulus. Look around by turning the head, not merely rolling the eyeballs. You might see somebody —in time.
3. Be extra careful before and during maneuvers that involve a rapid change of attitude or altitude. If you pull up beneath another pilot he surely will not see you in time to get out of your way. If you dive on him he might see you in time to get the full emotional bang out of the crash, but he wouldn't have time to dodge you. It usually requires only *one* unobservant pilot to cause a collision; the other pilot might never see what hit him.
4. Wear a parachute when there is other glider traffic in the vicinity. Caterpillar Club records and other sources indicate that over a quarter million lives have been saved by the big umbrella. Some of these were glider pilots, and a few of them were involved in mid-air collisions. Once again, the statistical chance is small, but—.

GROUND COLLISION

Mid-air collisions are indeed a statistical rarity, but the same cannot be said of ground collisions. If something is there to be run into, someone will run into it—sooner or later. An incomplete list of collidable objects includes cars, hangars, fences and boundary markers, people, and other gliders—*especially* other gliders.

Cross-wind take-offs and landings cause many "incidents." Better training, more experience, and a more cautious attitude seem to be required in this area. It is hard to teach a man how strong a side wind he can handle in any given glider; he must learn for himself, hopefully by easy stages. The limits for cross-wind take-offs must be learned the same way. When the cross-wind is severe, a pilot can hold one hand on the panel near the release knob, and at the first sign that he is losing directional control pull the release. An aborted take-off *without damage* is nothing to be ashamed of. Quite the contrary.

Most other ground collisions stem not from a lack of piloting skill or experience but from the mental attitudes of the pilot. Negligence does cause accidents through the pilot's failure to observe and plan while on the downwind leg, but this is a relatively minor factor. The *big* problem is the widely held idea that to miss an obstacle by inches reflects the pilot's keen judgment of distance and skillful control of the glider, whereas staying far from obstacles shows excessive caution and lack of confidence. When schools, clubs, and distinguished pilots work to change these attitudes the disgraceful record of ground accidents will be reduced. By precept *and* example the leaders of the soaring community can teach the newcomers that the need is not for show-offs or "Hero Pilots" but for those who demonstrate their skill and good judgment by staying *far* from trouble.

LOW ALTITUDE STALLS AND SPINS

Stalls and spins at low altitude are related causes of accidents, and are responsible for more pilot injuries and fatalities than all others combined. *Adequate airspeed would prevent all accidents from these two sources.*

If the above is true, why do pilots fly too slowly at low altitude? The only reasonable explanation is that they don't realize they are doing so. Higher up, they get used to thermaling at the brink of a stall, as they should. They recover from incipient stalls and spins quickly and with little loss of altitude simply by easing the stick forward a trifle. Consciously or not, they expect the glider to react in the same way when near the ground; usually it does. When it does *not,* there can be sad tidings.

What many pilots fail to realize is that the air in which they are flying close to the ground is behaving differently from the air higher up. Turbulence, thermal formation, gusts and lulls, and most common of all, the normal, predictable wind velocity gradient, are factors that change the flight behavior of the glider significantly. A sinking of the glider that might be unnoticed aloft could—on final approach—be excessively noticeable.

At the risk of repetitiousness, the matter of the wind velocity gradient will be re-stated. Too many hard landings have been caused by it to take the least chance that the reader does not get the message. The resistance to the wind offered by all manner of ground objects, trees, houses, hills, irregular terrain, almost anything, slows the wind near the ground. The height of the gradient is variable from a few feet to a few hundred feet. A pilot on final approach enters an area of lower headwind, perhaps as much as 10 to 15 mph less than he had a few seconds earlier. The glider sinks because the airflow across the wing is less than it was. Sinking increases the angle of attack; the wing may stall just where there isn't enough altitude for recovery.

Another effect of the wind gradient can occur when a pilot is turning steeply into the final approach at too low an airspeed, or (perish the thought) attempting to thermal two or three hundred feet above the ground. Yes, it does happen. If the pilot runs into the wind gradient as he is turning into the wind, it is easy to see that there will be less wind across the lower than the higher wing. The rolling force thus generated, because it is working on the entire wing area, can overpower the pilot's use of full aileron, rolling the glider past

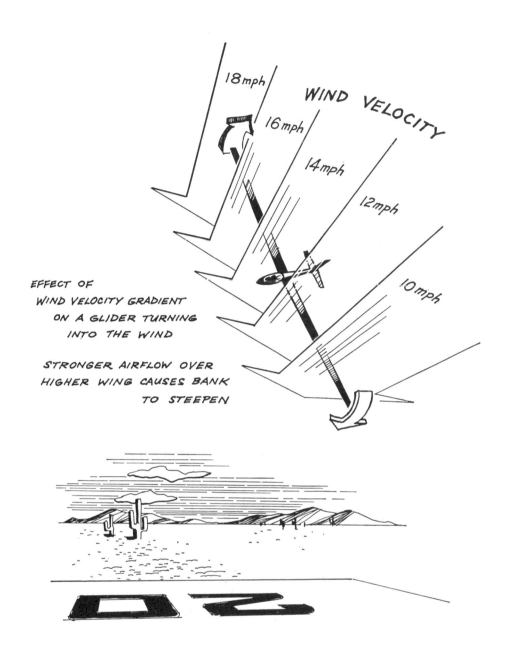

18mph

WIND VELOCITY

16mph

14mph

12mph

10mph

EFFECT OF
WIND VELOCITY GRADIENT
ON A GLIDER TURNING
INTO THE WIND

STRONGER AIRFLOW OVER
HIGHER WING CAUSES BANK
TO STEEPEN

a vertical bank. Gravity and adverse yaw pull the nose down. Without any warning buffet or shake, the glider simply fails to respond to the controls in time for recovery.

Some pilots actually abet these external contributory causes of spins at low altitude by making skidding turns when near the ground. This tendency could stem from a dislike of the banked attitude when flying low, or the fallacy about the rudder turning the glider like a boat. Whatever the reason, the skidding turn in conjunction with too-low airspeed and altitude is

very bad medicine indeed.

The desirability of spin instruction can hardly be overemphasized. At low altitude, the quick recognition and recovery such training gives are essential, second only to going fast enough to preclude these dire possibilities in the first place. No part of this manual has been the result of as much discussion and thought as the rule for pattern airspeed which is applicable to *any* glider: Fifty percent above the stalling speed plus half the estimated wind velocity. (Flaps up stalling speed, if applicable.)

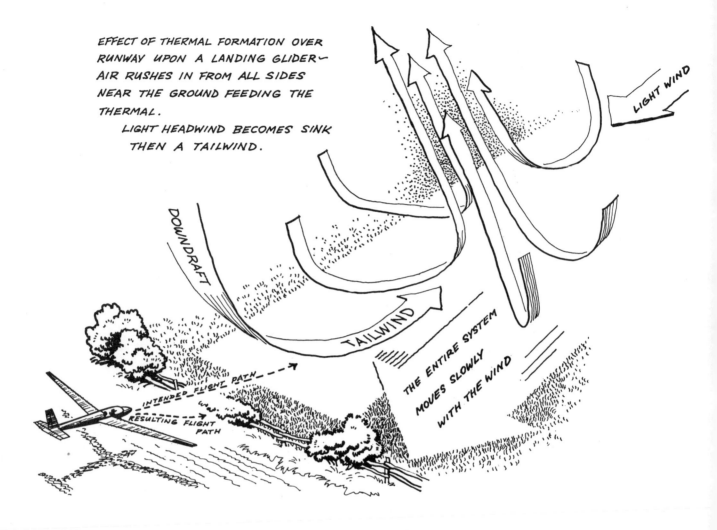

EFFECT OF THERMAL FORMATION OVER RUNWAY UPON A LANDING GLIDER—AIR RUSHES IN FROM ALL SIDES NEAR THE GROUND FEEDING THE THERMAL.

LIGHT HEADWIND BECOMES SINK THEN A TAILWIND.

LIGHT WIND

DOWNDRAFT

TAILWIND

INTENDED FLIGHT PATH

RESULTING FLIGHT PATH

THE ENTIRE SYSTEM MOVES SLOWLY WITH THE WIND

THERMAL FORMATION

Dirt airports and blacktop runways are excellent breeding places for thermals. These developing thermals are a serious threat to the pilot on final approach. As he nears the thermal he will first encounter strong sink, and a moment later the inrushing air which is feeding the thermal. The headwind to which he has adjusted his glide airspeed will quickly become a substantial tailwind, and the indicated airspeed will drop sharply, far worse than the usual effect of the wind gradient. The glider will sink rapidly and may not have enough altitude to regain flying speed.

When the pilot sees swirling dust, leaves or debris ahead, he has warning and should take instant action. He should close the spoilers and dive close to the ground to pick up airspeed. As soon as he is over the fence he should touch down at whatever speed, and while rolling try to stay out of the thermal. After coming to a stop he should stay in the glider, with spoilers open or flaps up, and brake on, until the thermal moves safely out of range.

When there is no visible indication of the thermal, the pilot will have to depend upon his correct pattern airspeed and his quickness in closing spoilers and nosing down. Glider pilots whose entire experience is in the relatively stable winter air should take heed. August has some surprises for January's students.

18. HEALTH CONSIDERATIONS

Applicants for glider pilot licenses are spared the expense of a physical examination and must only certify that they have no known defect that would render them unsafe to fly a glider. This policy puts the responsibility squarely on the pilot to be certain he meets the requirement. If there is the slightest doubt in his mind in this regard, the best procedure is to be examined by an FAA designated medical examiner who has special training and experience in the field of aviation medicine. The brief discussion which follows will help the applicant decide whether he should be examined, when it is better not to fly, and to learn about some factors that impair the efficiency of a pilot when he is already in the air.

Any ailment that might cause a person to be suddenly incapacitated is sufficient reason not to be a pilot. Examples are epilepsy, serious heart troubles, and some diabetic conditions; there are doubtless many others. Some temporarily disqualifying ailments are peptic ulcers, anemia, and acute infections.

There are causes other than serious disease that affect a pilot's ability to fly, to exercise good judgment, and as a student, to absorb instruction. One of these is the common cold. In addition to hampering the efficiency of the pilot, there is the danger of middle ear pain and of spreading the infection into the sinuses. Anything like a bad cold should ground a pilot until the symptoms abate.

Many medicines have an adverse effect on pilot efficiency. If under medication for any cause one should find out from any FAA medical examiner if the medicine is reason for grounding.

Habit-forming and hallucinogenic drugs and alcohol are out for pilots. So is flying when suffering from a hangover, even when the worst effects of it are masked by aspirin or other medication.

The SCUBA diver is well aware of the danger of the bends. He may not realize, however, that soaring soon after a dive can create a secondary hazard of the bends if the blood has not yet had time to normalize fully. The "diving pilot" should be aware of the possibility, and at the first sign of discomfort should descend to a more comfortable altitude.

Fatigue makes a poor student and a poor pilot. It is a waste of time and money to take flying lessons when just plain tired out. Fatigue is also an in-flight problem. Power pilots usually run out of gas before they run out of pep, but glider pilots don't run out of gas. A cross-country often lasts eight or ten hours, and at the end, when judgment is most needed, an exhausted pilot may be trying to decide where to land. He should be ultra-conservative in his planning and flying at such a time, knowing that neither his reflexes nor his judgment are as good as they were earlier.

Hypoxia is a shortage of oxygen in the blood, and glider pilots often reach an altitude where this occurs. The height at which hypoxia becomes serious depends first on altitude, then on the condition of the pilot, and finally on how long the pilot stays high. Alcohol and tobacco both reduce one's ability to withstand hypoxia. An early symptom may be an "I feel great! Altitude doesn't bother me!" feeling. Don't be fooled by the ecstasy of the heights. The Air Force has made thousands of tests to determine the extent of impairment of pilot faculties and judgment at altitude, the gist of which is that the pilot's ability to reason, plan, and make good decisions has been impaired long before headaches, fatigue or discomfort appear.

Because of the glider pilot's continuous need to think clearly and make decisions, it is wise to follow the example of the Air Force and breathe supplementary oxygen when above 10,000 feet ASL.

Airsickness is not too frequent among pilots because the control a pilot exerts over the glider eliminates the feeling of helplessness that is so much a part of seasickness. The pilot is *in charge,* and that makes all the difference. Some people with a tendency toward airsickness get over it after a few flights as they become more at home in the air. Alas, a few do not, and lose interest in soaring; others of weak stomach but stronger determination continue soaring but carry an airsickness bag. These are the authentic heroes of the sport.

The brilliant light encountered when flying soon converts most pilots to the wearing of sunglasses. In soaring, the polarizing type is especially valuable. With these glasses, when the head is tilted to the proper angle there is a pronounced darkening of the blue of the sky. Against this background, other gliders stand out more sharply, an obvious safety factor. The first appearance of wispy new cumulus cloud can be spotted earlier with polarizing glasses than with the naked eye. Some competition pilots claim that under certain conditions they can detect the presence of a thermal. These are all good things, but the prime reason for wearing sunglasses is still the protection they provide for the eyes, as attested by most aeromedical specialists.

19. GLIDER CARE

A glider pilot is quite likely to become a glider owner, and so ought to know a few things about caring for a sailplane. A safe storage practice is to keep the glider at home, in its covered trailer. Less safe is the open trailer, unless there is room for it in the garage, because of deterioration by weather and because aircraft possess a magnetic attraction for children.

At the airport, the best storage is in a locked hangar. There, the glider may be stored assembled, with canopy and pitot-static covers in place. A few gliderports provide hangar storage. When gliders are stored outside, the extent of hazards will depend on local conditions. Some deterioration from the elements is inevitable, instruments can be stolen and vandalism can occur.

With outside storage, secure tie-downs are essential. The FAA has published an excellent advisory (complete with harrowing photos of wind-damaged aircraft) showing how to install secure tie-downs. Note that the wing should be at a no-lift angle of attack. This is especially important for gliders, whose long wings have been known to buckle in a high wind at the point of "secure" tie-down. The actual tying of the wings should be with light tension, sufficient to prevent vertical play without straining the wing. All controls should be locked at the control surfaces, with red flags tied to the locks. Tying the cockpit controls in the glider is almost—but not quite—as secure as external locks of good design.

A canopy cover should be used to protect the plexiglass as well as to cover the ventilation duct and the pitot-static vents. In the event that the latter project, as on a trainer, a separate cover should be in place tied to the canopy cover with a stout cord so that both must be removed at the same time. Preflight inspections notwithstanding, both gliders and power planes have taken to the air with pitot covers still on. It makes for puzzling airspeed indications.

The inside surface of a cloth canopy cover should be kept scrupulously clean. If gritty with dust or blown sand it will scratch the plastic worse than if no cover were used. Dusty canopies should never be wiped with a dry cloth or paper, as fine scratches will result. The plexiglass should be flushed with running water (use a pitcher or a large squeeze-bottle) while gently wiping it with a piece of clean cheesecloth. When all the dust and grit are gone the canopy may be wiped dry *gently,* with more clean cheesecloth, to prevent water-spotting. If cared for with such tender solicitude, a canopy will remain like new for many years, providing safe forward vision when a landing must be made toward the setting sun.

The most satisfactory canopy cover is a home-made fibreglass job that rests on the fuselage and does not touch the plexiglass at any point. If it fits snugly around the edges, sealed with foam weatherstripping, it will reduce canopy washing to a minimum. Don't let "helpers" polish your canopy. They will wreck it in a hurry.

Because of heat and rain, instruments and radios do not fare well in a tied-down glider, even if they are not stolen. Some glider owners have them mounted in a quickly detachable panel or pedestal. The whole works can be removed in just a moment and stored at home in a dry, cool place.

When assembling a glider it is important to have some systematic way to check that all bolts, nuts and safety pins are in place. An assembly checklist is one way, but after a time one may cease to consult it. A better way is to make a small box with a separate compartment for each piece. A glance before assembly will show that all parts are there. If the box is empty when the job is done, it is fairly good assurance that everything is in place. When assembly is complete, a full-scale preflight inspection should be carried out to be doubly certain.

PART II – SOARING

20. THE PARACHUTE

There is a difference of opinion among soaring schools and clubs on the importance of wearing a parachute. Some schools are influenced by the unfortunate fact that an average sized instructor with parachute couldn't possibly get into or out of the back seat of some models of trainers. However, individual pilots should give consideration to the problem of *walking* back from a mid-air collision. It's easy, if you can also walk on water.

A parachute is required in all SSA sanctioned contests, and is customary in cross-country flights. In wave soaring, occasional rotor tur-

bulence can make a pilot feel the expense and bother of a parachute are worthwhile. Let's assume that every glider pilot will have occasion to wear a chute, and now provide the necessary minimum of information he should have when doing so.

The chute should be inspected before the pilot puts it on. It should be outwardly clean, dry and in good condition. The repacking record should be checked to be sure the chute is current; it will be found in a small pocket in the canvas pack. The back-pack chutes used by most glider pilots must have been repacked within the preceding 60 days. Next, the flap covering the pins should be opened and the pins and safety cord checked. The pins should be pushed fully into their studs, and the safety cord should be unbroken. The ripcord cable and housing should not have any sharp bends that could cause binding.

After inspection, the chute should be put on and the leg and chest straps pulled up tight while the pilot is standing. When he sits down they will be looser, but this is proper, and they should not be tightened further. In the case of a rental chute with which the pilot is not familiar, he should check the operation of the harness snaps on the chest and leg straps; there are both *regular* and *quick-release* types.

If it becomes necessary to bail out, the pilot should remember the possibility of the chute becoming fouled by some part of the glider, and try to be in the clear before pulling the ripcord. For this job, use two hands and pull *hard*. It is supposed to be good luck to hold on to the rip-cord. Perhaps the good luck consists of not having to buy another and not dropping it on someone's head.

A chute can be steered by pulling a shroud line on the side toward which one wishes to move. Air is spilled from the opposite side, causing the chute to glide sluggishly and to descend faster. When coming down in trees, keep your legs together. When landing on the ground, keep the knees slightly bent, and try to fall and roll to absorb the energy of the impact.

If there is enough surface wind to drag the pilot, he can collapse the parachute by pulling the riser nearest the ground. This is the moment to rejoice if your chute has the quick-release type harness snaps.

APPENDICES

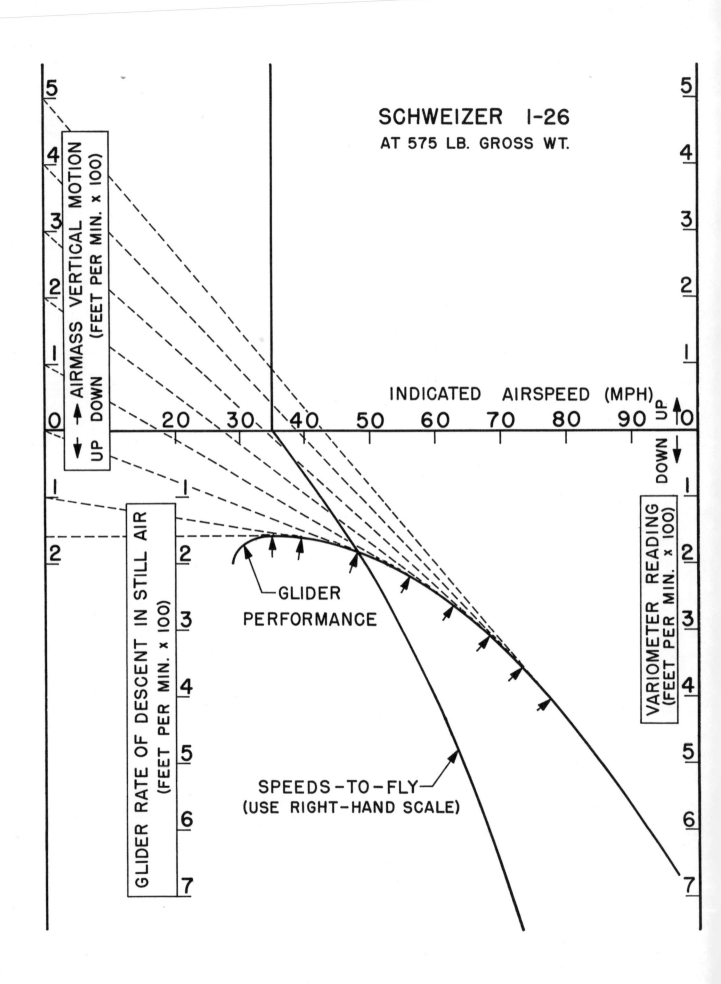

SCHWEIZER 1-26
AT 575 LB. GROSS WT.

AIRMASS VERTICAL MOTION (FEET PER MIN. × 100)

INDICATED AIRSPEED (MPH)

GLIDER RATE OF DESCENT IN STILL AIR (FEET PER MIN. × 100)

VARIOMETER READING (FEET PER MIN. × 100)

GLIDER PERFORMANCE

SPEEDS-TO-FLY (USE RIGHT-HAND SCALE)

CALCULATING SPEEDS-TO-FLY

Whenever a glider is in a descending air-mass the pilot should increase speed to escape from it with as little loss of altitude as possible. The question is *how fast* to fly.

It is a mathematical fact that in any given glider and condition of loading, the flattest glide possible for any indicated rate of descent (or best climb when the variometer reads plus) occurs at only one speed. Flying either faster or slower costs more altitude per mile. Therefore every pilot should have with him *in the glider* the speeds-to-fly of his ship at all variometer readings. The information may be displayed as a table or curve on an unused part of the instrument panel or better still, by plastic labels stuck around the bezel of the variometer.

The steps in calculating speeds-to-fly bring out the fact that flying a little too fast is less harmful to the glide ratio than flying the same amount too slow.

The only data needed to calculate speeds-to-fly is a performance curve of the glider. For our example in the following four steps we are using Schweizer Aircraft's curve for the 1-26 loaded to 575 lbs. gross weight.

1. Plot the performance curve on a very large sheet of graph paper. The axis of ordinates must pass through zero airspeed for the graphic solution to be correct. Note the three vertical scales, the left column appearing illogically upsidedown.

2. Draw tangents to the performance curve passing through the air-mass vertical motion scale as shown, one for each 100 fpm point and one horizontally through the high point of the curve, which is the point of minimum sink speed. Note carefully the exact points of tangency since these are the speeds-to-fly. They are marked with small arrows in the example.

3. At any instant, the variometer reading will be the algebraic sum of the air-mass vertical motion and the glider's rate of descent in still air for each point of tangency. Add the down motion, or subtract the up motion, to the rate of descent. This sum will be the variometer reading.

4. The resulting variometer reading is now plotted against the indicated airspeed, for example, at each point of tangency, and a smooth curve is drawn that ends at the speed for minimum sink. This is the speeds-to-fly curve which provides the information required by the pilot in the cockpit.

When flying, it will be found that the variometer reading and indicated airspeed are *convergent*. Suppose the glider is descending 200 fpm at 49 mph when sink is encountered and the variometer settles down at 400 fpm. The speeds-to-fly curve requires the pilot increase his speed to 60 mph. When he does so, the vario shows an increased rate of descent requiring a still higher airspeed. This could happen several times with diminishing discrepancies as the values converge. In practice, this is not a problem, as the pilot soon learns to overcorrect enough to find the proper airspeed for the increased rate of sink. In the example, he might fly at 65 mph and see if the vario stabilizes at 520 fpm as called for by the curve.

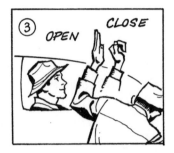

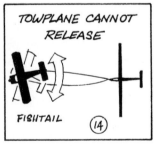

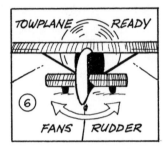

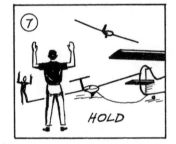

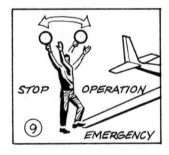

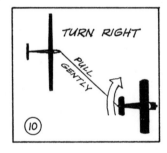

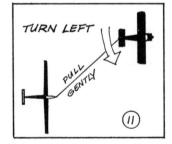

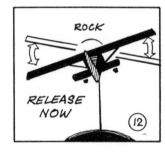

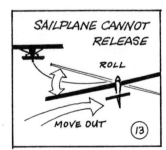

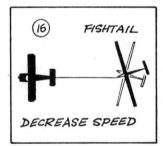

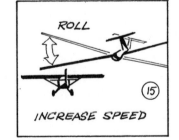

STANDARD AMERICAN SOARING SIGNALS

APPENDIX C

THE SOARING SOCIETY OF AMERICA'S ABC TRAINING PROGRAM

The ABC Training Program was set up at the behest of Society members to provide a standard of training. Its aim is to ensure that all students at participating schools and clubs receive complete and thorough instruction.

The levels of achievement attained by the student are recognized by the award of an A pin at solo, a B pin for proficiency in basic soaring flight and a C pin to mark readiness for cross-country flight. Further progress in the art of soaring is recognized by the FAI Badge program.

Requirements for the A pin

Preflight phase

Applicant has knowledge of:
1. Glider nomenclature
2. Glider handling procedures
3. Glider preflight check
4. Airport rules and Federal Aviation Regulations
5. Tow equipment signals and procedures
6. Hook-up of tow rope or cable
7. Take-off signals
8. Pilot responsibilities

Applicant holds:
1. Valid FAA student glider pilot certificate
2. Suitable log book

Presolo phase

Applicant has completed the following minimum flight training program:
1. Familiarization flight
2. Cockpit check procedure
3. Effects of controls, on the ground and in flight
4. Take-off procedure, cross-wind take-offs
5. Flight during tow
6. Straight glide
7. Simple turns
8. Circuit procedure and landing patterns
9. Landing procedure, downwind and cross-wind landings
10. Moderate and steep turns up to 720 degrees in both directions
11. Stalls and stall recovery
12. Conditions of spin entry and spin recovery
13. Effective use of spoilers/flaps and slips
14. Emergency procedures
15. Oral exam on Federal Aviation Regulations
16. Solo flight

Requirements for the B pin

Practice phase
1. Demonstration of soaring ability by solo flight of at least five minutes duration above point of release or starting point (low point after release), OR; thirty minutes duration after release from 2000' tow (add 1½ minutes /100' tow above 2000')

Requirements for the C pin

Precross-country phase
1. Dual soaring practice, including instruction in techniques for soaring thermals, ridges and waves (simulated flight and/or ground instruction may be used when suitable conditions do not exist)

2. Have knowledge of:
   a. Cross-country procedure recommended in the American Soaring Handbook (and this manual)
   b. Glider assembly, disassembly and retrieving
   c. Dangers of cross-country flying
3. Solo practice (two hours minimum)
4. Demonstration of ability to carry out simulated cross-country landings in restricted areas without reference to altimeter
5. Demonstration of soaring ability by solo flight of at least 30 minutes duration above point of release or starting point (low point after release), or 60 minutes duration after release from 2000' tow (add 1½ minutes/100' tow above 2000')

APPENDIX D

INTERNATIONAL SOARING AWARDS

One of the most interesting activities in the world of soaring is earning awards for accomplishments. These awards, called *Badges,* have great prestige because they are recognized standards of performance the world over.

The Badge system was established by the Fédération Aeronautique Internationale, the world governing body of aeronautical competition and record keeping. In this country the system is administered by the National Aeronautic Association (NAA) through its soaring division, the Soaring Society of America (SSA).

There are three levels of achievement honored by the award of the Silver Badge, the Gold Badge, and the Gold Badge with Diamonds, in ascending order. The latter is often loosely referred to as the Diamond Badge. Detailed rules for the conduct of award flights (subject to change from time to time) are available from SSA. The general conditions, omitting much "fine print", are as follows:
1. Every flight must be supervised by an SSA Official Observer.
2. The pilot must be alone in the aircraft.
3. A sealed barograph must be carried on all flights except for duration when the Official Observer attests that he watched the entire flight.
4. Distance flights with a turn point must have an Official Observer witness the turn, or the pilot may photograph the turn point from the air.
5. Only two tests for any one badge are permitted on any one flight, except in the case of the Gold Badge with Diamonds, for which all of the tests may be made in one flight.

The Silver Badge requires three tasks:

A flight of at least 5 hours duration.
A flight of at least 50 kilometers in a straight line.
A height gain of at least 1000 meters.

The Gold Badge requires three tasks:

A flight of at least 5 hours duration, which may be the same flight as for the Silver Badge.
A distance flight of 300 kilometers.
A height gain of at least 3000 meters.

A Diamond may be added to the Gold Badge for each of the following tasks:

A flight to a pre-declared goal of 300 kilometers.
A distance flight of 500 kilometers.
A height gain of 5000 meters.

The 300 and 500 kilometer flights may be made either in a straight line, a triangle, a goal-and-return, or a dog-leg with one turning point. Distance flights are subject to penalty under a formula when the altitude lost between release and landing is over 1000 meters.

There are rumors at the time of writing of changes in the tasks or rules for Badge flights, so the reader is cautioned to secure up-to-date rules from the SSA.

APPENDIX E

SUGGESTED READING LIST

Copies of the following are available from Soaring Society of America, Inc., Box 66071, Los Angeles, Calif. 90066.

Soaring, the journal of the SSA, a monthly, free to all members.

American Soaring Handbook, published by SSA in ten chapters, with a binder available for the complete series. Each chapter is a separate booklet treating the title subject fully.

Chapter

1 *A History of American Soaring,* by Ralph S. Barnaby.
2 *Training,* by William R. Fuchs. This is a syllabus for SSA's training program.
3 *Ground Launch,* by William R. Fuchs.
4 *Airplane Tow,* by Tom Page.
5 *Meteorology* by Harner Selvidge.
6 *Cross-Country* and *Wave Soaring* by Richard H. Johnson and William S. Ivans respectively.
7 *Equipment I, Instruments and Oxygen,* by Harner Selvidge.
8 *Equipment II, Radio, Rope and Wire,* by John D. Ryan and Harold Drew.
9 *Aerodynamics,* not yet available.
10 *Maintenance and Repair,* by Robert Forker.

The following books, all of the greatest value to soaring pilots, are available at most glider schools and clubs, and elsewhere.

Meteorology for Glider Pilots, by C. E. Wallington.
Gliding, by Derek Piggott.
Cloud Study, by Ludlam and Scorer.
Soaring for Diamonds, by Joseph C. Lincoln.
New Soaring Pilot, by Ann & Lorne Welch and Frank Irving.

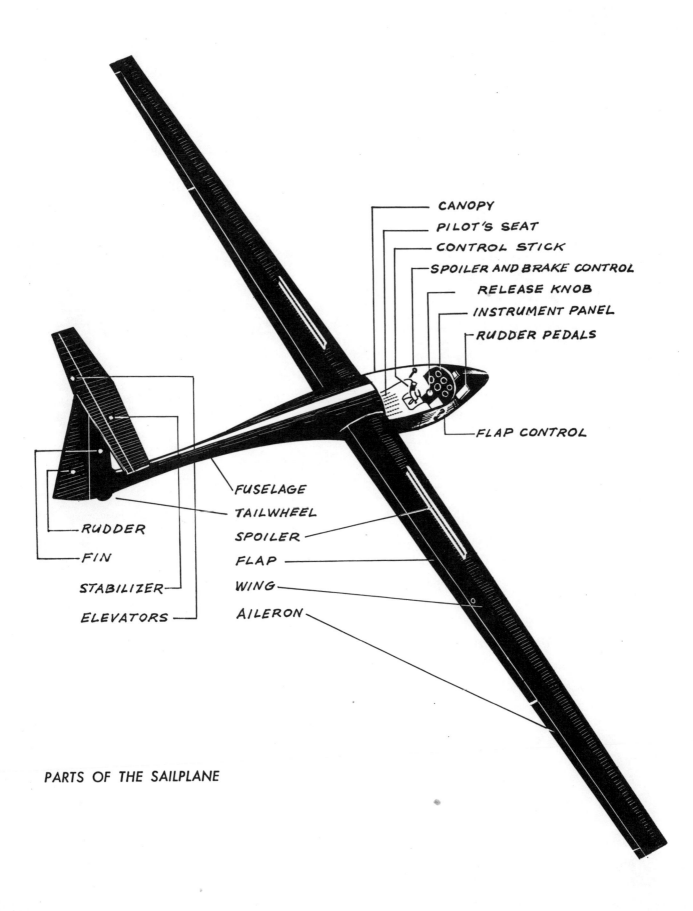

CANOPY

PILOT'S SEAT

CONTROL STICK

SPOILER AND BRAKE CONTROL

RELEASE KNOB

INSTRUMENT PANEL

RUDDER PEDALS

FLAP CONTROL

FUSELAGE

TAILWHEEL

SPOILER

FLAP

WING

AILERON

RUDDER

FIN

STABILIZER

ELEVATORS

PARTS OF THE SAILPLANE

GLOSSARY

Accelerated Stall — A stalled angle of attack of the wing at an airspeed above the minimum for that condition. Also called a high-speed stall. Deliberate accelerated stalls are a prelude to all snap-type aerobatic maneuvers.

AGL — Above ground level (altitude).

Aileron — A hinged portion of the trailing edge of the wing near the tip that is used to provide a banking or rolling force around the glider's longitudinal axis.

Airfoil — Any part of an aircraft (primarily the wing and tail surfaces) which deflects the air through which it moves so as to produce a useful reaction upon itself.

Airspeed — The speed of an aircraft in relation to the air through which it is flying. *Indicated* airspeed (IAS) is the reading of the airspeed indicator. *True* airspeed (TAS) is the IAS corrected for air density, so far as glider pilots are concerned. Test personnel also include a factor of calibration for instrumental and installation errors, of no concern in day-to-day gliding.

Airworthiness Certificate — A record of the date of the most recent annual inspection; it must be displayed openly in the glider.

Anabatic Wind — The rising air close to the surface of a sun-facing slope. This thin layer of lift is quite unlike the common thermal.

Angle of Attack — The acute angle between the mean chord of the wing and the direction in which it moves through the air. The angle of attack is independent of the attitude of the glider with respect to the horizon and could have the same value in a straight glide, a vertical bank or at the top of a loop.

Angle of Incidence — The acute angle between the mean chord of the wing and the longitudinal axis of the glider.

ASL — Above sea level (altitude).

Aspect Ratio — The ratio between the glider's span and the mean chord of its wings. High aspect ratio in a glider is associated with a high glide ratio, other factors being equal.

Attitude — The inclination of the axes of the glider to the horizontal.

Axis — The theoretical line extending through the center of gravity of a glider in each major plane. The three axes are: longitudinal, or fore and aft; lateral, or crosswise; and vertical, or up and down.

Bank — To tip or roll about the longitudinal axis of the glider. Banks are necessary to all properly executed turns. In gliding, banks are classified as shallow (0-20 deg.), medium (20-45 deg.), and steep (over 45 deg.). This classification differs from that of power flight.

Barograph — A recording aneroid barometer. A calibration chart showing elevation in the standard atmosphere must be used in conjunction with the barograph. A barograph is required equipment for Badge and Record flights. A recording of a flight is called a barogram.

Barrel Roll — An aerobatic maneuver in which the aircraft rolls 360 degrees while describing a helix around a horizontal axis. The roll is produced by continuous up elevator and coordinated aileron and rudder.

Best Glide Speed — The indicated airspeed that results in the flattest glide obtainable in perfectly still air.

Buffeting — The beating effect on the rear of a glider caused by the turbulent wake of the wing as the angle of attack nears the stalling point. Buffeting warns the pilot of the approach of the stall, normally becoming stronger as the angle of attack increases further. The initial buffeting does not mean the wing is stalled, merely that separation has begun at the trailing edge. Different tail configurations change the buffeting characteristics of sailplanes.

Camber — The cross-sectional curvature of the wing.

Catabatic Wind — The downslope or drainage wind caused by radiation cooling of a shaded slope. It is similar in form to the anabatic wind, lying close to the slope.

Center of Gravity — The point within a glider through which, for balance purposes, the total force of gravity is considered to act.

Chandelle — An aerobatic maneuver consisting of a 180 degree climbing turn that terminates on the verge of a stall.

Checkpoint — In aerial navigation, an easily identifiable spot on the ground, (and on the map) used to mark the progress of a flight.

Chord — The line of a straightedge brought into contact with the lower surface of an airfoil section at two points. In the case of an airfoil having double convex camber, it is a straight line joining the leading and trailing edges.

Clean — The condition of a glider after reducing parasitic drag to the lowest possible value. The opposite of "dirty," naturally.

Clear (the area) — This special use of an overworked word means to verify that the nearby airspace is *clear* of other aircraft. Steeply banked *clearing turns* are necessary before and during rapid descent.

Convection — The up or down movement of a limited portion of the atmosphere. The term usually refers to thermal action.

Convergence — The area where two bodies of air that have relative motion meet. A likely area of lift.

Coordination — The use of aileron and rudder in such a way that the glider neither slips nor skids; i.e., the slip-skid ball and the yaw string remain centered.

Course — The ground path over which the pilot intends to fly. *True* course is measured by reference to the meridians of longitude on a map. *Magnetic* course is TC corrected for variation. *Compass* course is MC corrected for deviation.

Crabbing — Pointing the glider somewhat up-wind so as to counteract for wind drift. Crab angle is also called wind correction angle.

Crossed Controls — Simultaneous application of right rudder and left aileron or vice versa. Crossed controls are used to produce slips and skids; however, in a normal turn some degree of crossed controls may be needed to overcome the slipping caused by the higher induced drag of the faster-moving wing.

Cross-country Speed — The actual point-to-point speed after taking into account any difference in altitude ASL of the glider over the two points. If the altitude factor is ignored the calculation can be grossly incorrect and meaningless. Cross-country speed is of most interest in post-flight analysis. Its navigational value is nil because it is changing constantly.

Cumulonimbus (CuNim) — The thunderhead, in all its majesty.

Cumulus — A cloud whose origin is in upward-moving air. Vertical development is aided by the appearance of latent heat of condensation.

Decay — The stage in the life cycle of a cumulus cloud when the lift has changed to sink. The cloud is evaporating, cooling the air. Rain showers are often present, and the base of the cloud appears ragged.

Deviation — The compass error caused by local magnetic forces in the glider.

Dive Brakes — Devices whose prime purpose is to create drag; most dive brakes also reduce lift.

Diving Tendency — The tendency in a turn for the nose to fall and the airspeed to increase.

Downwash — The downward thrust imparted to the air by a wing, whose "equal and opposite reaction" supports the aircraft.

Drag — The force opposing the forward motion of the glider (wind resistance, to plain folks). Drag is of two kinds. *Induced* drag of the wings is the component of the aerodynamic reaction that is parallel to the direction of motion of the glider through the surrounding air. *Parasitic* drag is the drag of a glider that is not productive of lift.

Drift — The angle between a glider's heading and track.

Elevator — The horizontal movable surface at the tail used to control the angle of attack of the wing.

Empennage — The entire tail group of an aircraft, consisting of fixed and movable elements.

Fairing — A member or structure whose primary purpose is to smooth the airflow over the aircraft to reduce drag.

Federal Aviation Administration (FAA) — The governing body of civil aviation in the U.S. Its responsibility in the field of soaring includes the airworthiness of gliders, licensing of pilots and gliders, air traffic rules, and many other matters.

Fédération Aeronautique Internationale (FAI) — The world governing body of aeronautical contests and custodian of world records.

Fin — The fixed vertical tail surface, used to provide directional stability.

Flaps — Hinged portions of the trailing edge of both wings between the ailerons and the fuselage, whose purpose is to alter the lift and drag characteristics of the wing.

Flare (out) — In landing, to change the final approach flight path from descending to parallel with the landing surface. *Round out* is also used with the same meaning.

Floater — A glider with low wing loading, low minimum speed and low rate of sink. The opposite of a *lead sled*.

Foehn Gap — In a mountain wave system marked by clouds, the foehn gap is an area of blue sky between the mountain's cap clouds and the lenticular cloud over the first lee wave.

Foehn Wind — A warm dry wind blowing down the slope of a mountain. The Chinook, of the Rocky Mountains, is one of many local names given to foehn winds.

"G" — For gravity, of course. The load on a glider's structure is stated in terms of multiples of the force of gravity. A 4G load on a wing would be four times the load applied by gravity alone.

Glide — Sustained forward flight in which speed is maintained by descending in the surrounding air. A glider gains altitude only by descending in upward-moving air that is rising faster than the glider's rate of descent.

Glider (Sailplane) — Any wing-supported aircraft with no power source of its own. Glider and sailplane are usually used synonymously. When a distinction is intended, sailplanes are meant for soaring whereas gliders are primarily for descent.

Glide Ratio — The ratio of forward to downward motion, numerically the same as the ratio of lift to drag, L/D.

Ground Effect — The gain in lift during flight close to the ground that is caused by compression of the air between the wings and the ground, by interference of the ground with the airflow patterns about the wing, and other factors. It is greatest as close to the ground as possible, but is measurable up to an altitude equal to the glider's wingspan.

Ground Loop — An uncontrollable violent turn on the ground.

Ground Speed — The glider's speed with reference to the earth. It is the true airspeed plus or minus the effect of the wind.

Hang-glider — A pioneer type glider in which the pilot was supported by his shoulders and arms, his body hanging below the glider. Control was by the pilot shifting his weight.

Heading — The direction the pilot is aiming the glider. In navigation, the course corrected for wind drift. Heading may be true, magnetic or compass.

High Tow (Normal Tow) — In aero tow, the position of the glider slightly above the towplane's wake. It is *not* high with respect to the towplane itself.

Horizontal Wind Shear — A change in wind velocity or direction with altitude. An example of special concern to glider pilots is the *wind velocity gradient*.

Isogonic Line — On maps, a line connecting points of equal magnetic variation. They are used when computing magnetic course from true course.

Knot — A unit of speed equalling one nautical mile (6080 feet) per hour. The phrase *knots per hour* is improper—there is no such thing.

Landing Speed — The indicated airspeed at the moment of touchdown. If ground speed is intended, the term should be qualified.

Lapse Rate — In the atmosphere, the rate of change of temperature with altitude.

L/D (spoken L over D) — Lift divided by drag. This significant ratio is numerically the same as the glide ratio. The maximum L/D of a glider is widely and erroneously accepted as the summation of a glider's merit—primarily because numerical values cannot be placed on other important qualities. But a high L/D is important.

Lazy Eight — A mild aerobatic maneuver developed from a pair of 180 degree turns in opposite directions. Climbs and dives alternate. Easy to do; hard to do well.

Leading Edge — The forward edge of an airfoil—the opposite of trailing edge.

Lead Sled — Slang for the high-performance sailplane with high wing-loading. It achieves a fast flat glide at a sacrifice of some thermaling ability in weak conditions.

Lenticular Cloud (Lennie) — The characteristic cloud of a lee wave. See the section on wave flying for description and illustration.

Lift — (1) Upward currents strong enough to carry a glider up. (2) Loosely, the supporting force of a wing. More accurately, the force acting perpendicularly to the path of flight of an airfoil.

Load — The forces acting on the structure of a glider. *Static* load is the weight of the glider. *Gross* load is the ready-to-fly weight, pilot included. *Maneuvering* loads are those imposed by use of the controls, and *gust* loads are those imposed by air currents. The *useful* load is the difference between the empty weight and the maximum authorized weight.

Load Factor — The sum of the loads on a structure, expressed in G units. The *limit* load factor is the pilot's *never exceed* value, beyond which structural damage may occur. The *ultimate* load factor (1.5 times the limit load factor) is the load at which to expect structural *failure*.

Log — A required record of pilot or glider flight time. Details are covered by FAA regulations.

Loop — An aerobatic maneuver as nearly as possible a perfect circle in a vertical plane. (Commonly, more like a longhand letter L.) It may be inside or outside. In the latter, the top of the aircraft is on the outside of the circle, and since the stresses on both pilot and glider are severe, the maneuver is not recommended.

Low Tow — In aero tow, the position of the glider slightly below the towplane's wake.

MacCready Speed Ring — A rotatable bezel around the variometer marked with the indicated airspeed suitable to various rates of climb or descent. When the index is placed opposite the point of zero sink on the variometer, the needle points to the I.A.S. which gives the flattest glide. When the pilot wishes to sacrifice flattest glide in favor of the highest cross-country speed, he "guesstimates" the average rate of climb he will make good in the *next* thermal and then rotates the bezel so the index falls opposite this rate of climb. He then flies at the airspeed indicated on the bezel by the variometer needle. If his guess turns out correct he will make good the highest possible cross-country speed. Dr. Paul MacCready, the inventor of the speed ring which bears his name, is exceptionally well-qualified to prophesy the strength of the next thermal.

Maneuvering Speed — The maximum speed at which the controls can be fully and abruptly applied without damage to the glider structure. The maneuvering speed may be indicated on the placard and will certainly be given in the flight manual for the glider. This speed is also the safe maximum in severe turbulence.

Minimum Sink Speed — The indicated airspeed at which the glider loses altitude most slowly. Minimum sink speed will be found at the crest of the performance curve a few mph above stalling speed and moderately below best glide speed.

National Aeronautic Association (NAA) — The U.S. national aero club. The body delegated by the FAI to govern aeronautical contests and process record claims in the U.S. For soaring, this work has been re-delegated to SSA, a division of NAA.

Open-class Gliders — Unrestricted, within the competitive definition of the term *glider*. Any span, fuselages scaled to midget pilots, anything goes.

OSTIV — Organisation Scientifique et Technique du Vol a Voile. (V.aV. is French for gliding.) OSTIV publishes papers on the technical aspects of meteorology, training, soaring techniques, gliders and equipment. It is affiliated with the FAI. OSTIV developed the specifications for Standard Class gliders, and conducts periodic design contests to honor the best in this class.

Overbanking Tendency — In a turn, the effect of the outer wing going faster than the inner wing and thus having more lift, steepening the angle of bank.

Overdevelopment — An increase in the extent of cumulus cloud cover which significantly reduces the sun's heating of the earth, slowing or even stopping thermal activity.

Overshoot — To land beyond the intended spot—the opposite of undershoot.

Penetrate — To make progress against an adverse wind. Good penetration requires the glider to have a good glide ratio in the upper speed range.

Pitch Attitude — The angle of the longitudinal axis of the glider to the horizontal. Nose high or low.

Pitot Tube — An open-ended tube exposed to the air in front of the glider for measuring impact air pressure. The pitot tube is the source of dynamic pressure for the airspeed indicator and the constant energy device of the variometer.

Placard — A required statement of operation limitations that is permanently affixed where it can be seen by the pilot during flight.

Porpoising — Repeated dynamic pitching of the glider when being ground launched.

Red Line — A warning red mark on the airspeed indicator that corresponds to the maximum airspeed given on the placard.

Registration Certificate — Statement of ownership and assigned identity numbers of the glider. It must be displayed where it can be seen when the glider is on the ground.

Release — The device for, or the act of, disengaging the tow rope.

Rollout — The path of a landing glider after it touches down until it comes to a full stop.

Rotor — The swirling circulation under a lee wave. The rotor is sometimes marked by ragged wispy clouds and is an area of severe turbulence.

Roundover — In a ground launch, the period just before release, when the rate of climb is diminishing and the glider is resuming a normal gliding attitude.

Rudder — The hinged vertical control surface that is used to induce or overcome yawing moments about the vertical axis. It resembles a boat's rudder, but its purpose and use are quite different.

Sea Breeze Front — The zone of convergence between warm inland air and the moist cool air from over the ocean.

Separation — Turbulence over the top of an airfoil. Burble.

Shear Line — The plane of separation between air masses moving at different speeds or in different directions. The shear may be vertical, horizontal, or inclined.

Shot Down — Unable to remain aloft. The term implies that conditions were at fault rather than piloting ability.

Sink — Descending currents in which the glider loses altitude faster than in still air.

Skid — Sideways motion of a glider with wings level; or in a turn, away from the low wing.

Slip — Sideways motion of a glider toward the lowered wing.

Slip-skid Ball — An instrument to detect slips and skids, thus helping the pilot to fly in a coordinated manner. It consists of a curved glass tube containing a metal ball. The pilot tries to fly so the ball remains in the center of the tube in all normal maneuvers. See also *Yaw String*.

Slow Flight — A required part of the FAA glider pilot flight test. See text for details.

Slow Roll — An aerobatic maneuver wherein ailerons are used for rolling while rudder and elevators are used to keep the fuselage aimed at a point on or slightly above the horizon. Not recommended.

Snap Roll — An aerobatic maneuver consisting of an abrupt one-turn spin around a horizontal axis. Entry is from an accelerated stall at *less* than maneuvering speed.

Soar — To fly without engine power and without loss of altitude.

Soaring Society of America (SSA) — A division of the National Aeronautic Association, the SSA is the delegated governing body for soaring contests and record flights in the U.S., publishes SOARING Magazine and other publications, and represents the interests of the sport before the regulatory agencies of government. Acts as coordinator, supporter and friend to all segments of soaring, both private and commercial. SSA operates with a small paid staff and a vast amount of volunteer effort from its more dedicated members. SSA can always use more such help.

Span — The maximum distance from wingtip to wingtip of an aircraft.

Speed-to-Fly — The indicated airspeed which produces the flattest glide in any situation of convection without considering the effect of wind. See Appendix A.

Spin — An aerobatic maneuver in which the glider spirals tightly downward in a nose-low attitude, the inner wing being stalled.

Spiral — All gliding turns are generally spiral in form. The unintended and uncontrolled high-speed spiral can be dangerous, so is fully covered in the text.

Spoilers — Devices that disturb the airflow across the wing to *spoil* the lift and increase drag. The lower value of L/D results in a steeper glide path.

Stability — The tendency of the glider, without action by the pilot, to maintain a normal straight glide and to return to this condition if the glider's attitude is disturbed.

Stable Air — An atmosphere with a lapse rate such that a parcel of air which is displaced up or down will tend to return to its original level.

Stabilizer — The fixed horizontal tail surface used to provide pitch stability.

Stall — The abrupt loss of lift at the angle of attack at which the flow of air separates significantly from the top of the wing rather than being deflected downward. An aircraft can be stalled in any attitude, and the only way to unstall it is to reduce the angle of attack, i.e., *move the stick forward.*

Stalling Speed — The airspeed at which the wing stalls in a steady straight glide with no gust or maneuvering loads. The term is sometimes qualified to indicate the speed of stalling under other conditions.

Standard Class Glider — A class of glider established by OSTIV. Specifications are aimed at moderate cost, safety, comfort, and good handling qualities. Span is limited to 15 meters.

Static Source — A source of air at the surrounding atmospheric pressure, unaffected by dynamic forces. In actual practice it is very difficult to locate such a source in a glider. Any dynamic pressures that intrude in the static system will affect the accuracy of the airspeed indicator, the altimeter and the variometer, all of which may be operated from the same static source.

Stick — The control within the cockpit that actuates the ailerons and elevator.

Terminal Velocity — The highest speed attainable in a prolonged vertical dive. Drag producing devices may be used to hold terminal velocity below placard maximum.

Thermal — Air heated by the underlying surface rising through surrounding cooler air. Thermals may also be triggered when unstable air is lifted by other means, for example, by cold fronts. *Thermaling* is climbing in a thermal.

Total Energy Variometer — A variometer which has been compensated so as to respond only to changes in the total energy of the sailplane; thus a change in airspeed due to stick deflection does not register as lift or sink on the variometer.

Track — The ground path over which the glider actually flies. See also *course*. Course is the pilot's intention; track is his accomplishment, which may be quite different.

Triggering Time and Temperature — The time and temperature at which useful thermals begin.

Trimmer — A small auxiliary control on the elevator of a glider, or a spring device bearing on the elevator control system, for the purpose of relieving the pilot of the need to hold a pressure on the stick to maintain his desired airspeed.

Variation — The compass error caused by the difference in location of the earth's true and magnetic north poles.

Variometer — A sensitive and fast-responding instrument showing rate of climb or descent. The basic instrument of soaring.

Wake — The disturbed and mostly downward moving air behind an aircraft.

Weak Link — A section of rope of a breaking strength specified by the FAA that is incorporated into stronger tow ropes and cables as a safety device.

Wetted Area — The external surface area of a glider. Some modern designs have very small fuselages aft of the cockpit to reduce the wetted area, and hence minimize the parasitic drag of the glider.

Wind Shadow — An area of calm in the lee of windbreaks such as hills, buildings and rows of trees. Such spots, when sunny, are likely sources of thermals on windy days.

Wind Shift — An abrupt change in the surface wind that can pose a serious problem for any landing aircraft, but especially for gliders.

Wind Velocity Gradient — The horizontal wind shear close to the ground caused by the frictional effect of the terrain. The gradient can be a hazard to landing gliders, so is discussed fully in the chapter on *Safety*, subsection on *Low Altitude Stalls and Spins*.

Wing — An airfoil whose major function is to provide lift by the dynamic reaction of the mass of air swept downward.

Wing-over — An aerobatic maneuver for effecting a reversal of direction with a minimum turning radius. The glider is pulled up to a very steep pitch attitude straight ahead. When the speed is very low, full rudder is applied to yaw the glider 180 degrees around its vertical axis (beware a tail slide, for which the glider might not be stressed). Now, pointing nearly straight down, the glider accelerates and is brought back to normal glide attitude.

Yaw — Rotation of the glider around its vertical axis. *Adverse yaw* is against the direction of banking and is caused by the difference in drag of the down and up ailerons.

Yaw string — A few inches of yarn tied to the top of the pitot-static head of a trainer, or similar mast on other gliders. When it blows to one side it indicates a slip or a skid. When a yaw string is taped to the windshield, the dividing airflow around the canopy results in wildly exaggerated yaw string action.